W9-BGN-606

If you sometimes feel lonely
    even when surrounded by people,
if you long to have a deep friendship with another woman
    but don't know how,
if you bear wounds from your relationship with your mother
    and need healing,
if you are a mother and want a close, warm, and secure friendship
    with your child,
then this book is for you!

Susan Alexander Yates, mother of five and author of *And Then I Had Kids* and *What Really Matters at Home*

Dr. Brenda Hunter's new book, *In the Company of Women,* is a vital look at the importance of female relationships. It explains why I've found my two daughters and my daughter-in-law to be my best friends and why I've gained incredible support and friendship from other women. It is a powerful motivator to make oneself available as a friend to other women. I highly recommend this book!

Joanne Kemp

My life has been greatly enriched by Brenda Hunter's research and helpful insights on mother-daughter relationships. Her new book, *In the Company of Women,* provides powerful testimony to our need for nurturing and being nurtured throughout our lives—in our friendships as well as in our family relationships. Were we to heed her challenges on mentoring and mothering, our society would be transformed.

Linda LeSourd Lader
President, Renaissance Institute

In the Company of Women addresses one of the real problems of our day: the inability of major portions of our society to enjoy rich, God-created intimacy. My heart spilled over with gratitude as the chapters on mothers and daughters confirmed all that my single-parent mom did right. Other chapters challenged me to work on some relationships that are bursting with promise but are, as yet, unfulfilled. This is a book I am going to give to the most important women in my life, and I commend it to you as well.

Colleen Townsend Evans

In the Company of WOMEN

In the Company of WOMEN

Deepening our relationships with the important women in our lives...mothers, daughters, sisters, friends & mentors

Brenda Hunter, Ph.D.

MULTNOMAH BOOKS

IN THE COMPANY OF WOMEN
© 1994 by Brenda Hunter, Ph.D.

published by Multnomah Books
a part of the Questar publishing family

International Standard Book Number: 0-88070-839-5 (pa)

Cover illustration by Leslie Wu
Cover design by David Carlson

Printed in the United States of America

Scripture quotations are from the *Revised Standard Version of the Bible*,
copyright 1946, 1952, 1971, 1973, Division of Christian Education,
National Council of the Churches of Christ in the USA.
Used by permission.

The illustrations and stories in this book are based on actual situations,
but the names, locations, and circumstances have been changed
when necessary to protect the identity of the individuals.

ALL RIGHTS RESERVED
No part of this publication may be reproduced, stored in a retrieval system,
or transmitted, in any form or by any means—
electronic, mechanical, photocopying, recording, or otherwise—
without prior written permission.

For information:
QUESTAR PUBLISHERS, Inc.
Post Office Box 1720
Sisters, Oregon 97759

Library of Congress Cataloging-in-Publication Data
Hunter, Brenda.
    In the company of women/Brenda Hunter.
        p.   cm.
    ISBN 0-88070-633-5
    1. Women--Psychology. 2. Interpersonal relations. 3. Mothers and daughters.
        4. Friendship. I. Title
HQ1206.H86 1984   94-21369
158.2--dc20   CIP

97 98 99 00 01 02 03 04— 14 13 12 11 10 9 8 7

To the young women closest to my heart—
my daughters, Holly and Kristen.

Contents

Introduction..17

1. The Necessary Company of Women 19
2. Mother: Our First Connection.....................................31
3. Mother Love..45
4. Mother Woe..55
5. Making Peace with Our Mothers 69
6. Daughters: Our Mirror Images 81
7. The Sister Knot...97
8. Women and Friendship..109
9. Key Players and Second Stringers...............................121
10. The Art of Friendship..131
11. Surviving Conflict in Friendships..............................145
12. Friendship's End...157
13. When Men Aren't Enough...165
14. Mentors: Passing the Torch.......................................179
15. My Mentor/Myself..195
16. The Legacy..205
17. Epilogue 213

Notes 217

Acknowledgments

While few probably read the Acknowledgments, I hope that those who provided encouragement and practical help in the writing of this book will allow me publicly to say "thank you."

To Don, my husband. This is the fifth book you've read, edited, and encouraged me to write. As ever, you've been tremendously supportive and you've believed in me. Thank you, Don. I owe much to your kindness and practical help. Let's keep working together on books—yours as well as mine.

To my daughter, Holly. I depend on your savvy, your editorial comments, and your computer genius. You truly are a writing colleague, and I'm grateful for all the ideas you suggested, especially in the area of friendship. I'll keep the note you wrote that last weekend as we pushed to finish—the note from the "maternally shackled." I hope to see you in print soon, my zany, literary daughter. Thanks, Hol.

To my editor, Carol Bartley. Thank you for your excitement about this project and for your fine editorial comments. As we have talked about the book over the months, we've become friends. For that, I'm grateful. Carol, I appreciate your sense of humor, your honesty, and the way you turn my occasional psychobabble into clear sentences.

This book could not have been written without the stories friends shared, the questionnaires some fifty women took the time to fill out, and the inclusion of personal accounts from other writers. Thanks to the writers from *Welcome Home* magazine who agreed to allow me to use their published stories. And I am deeply grateful to friends who took time to write a piece when I called up at the last minute and needed their help. Their voices add much depth and texture to this book. Thanks to Karen Henry, Sherry Von Ohlsen, Heidi Brennan, Kristie Tamillow, Pam Goresh, and Scott McMichael. (Scott, I'm sure you're delighted to be the only male in such an auspicious gathering of female writers!)

I am also indebted to all those individuals who gave of their time for the interviews that enrich this book, especially Dr. David Allen, Novie Hinson, Linda LeSourd Lader, Megan Beyer, Dru Ramey, Anne-Marie McMichael, Susan Yates, Jennifer Leber, and the women of the Owen family.

Lastly, many, many thanks to those dear friends who prayed for me and encouraged me when I needed it: Sue Leach, Kristie Tamillow, Eleanor Carr, and Georgie Eddins.

*Oh, the comfort—the inexpressible comfort of feeling
safe with a person, having neither to weigh thoughts,
nor measure words—but pouring them all out—
just as they are—chaff and grain together—
certain that a faithful hand will take and sift them—
keep what is worth keeping—
and with the breath of kindness blow the rest away.*

Dinah Craik

Introduction

I have just come from a gathering of women. For three hours this morning the four of us sat in a local restaurant, sharing our needs, our concerns, our unanswered questions—our hearts. Two of us cried after deep confessionals; all of us laughed. I'm sure the waiter thought we were nuts as we laughed even while tears streamed down our faces. But that's the way women are. We cry in front of our closest friends, assured we're in a safe place, and we sometimes laugh through our tears. In fact, laughter eases our hurting hearts.

When it was time to go—as other commitments called—we ran outside into the spring rain, lighthearted as children out for recess, and jumped into one car. For a few moments we prayed—for each other and for ourselves—thanking God for bringing us together in the first place, for giving us to each other as friends.

Friends. Relationships. For women that's what life's about. We are relational beings. As such, we almost always put our relationships with husbands, children, and friends before ambition and material gain. Yet the evidence is that our life-nourishing relationships are being eroded today as we live frenetic, time-pressured lives. Moreover, we have just come through three decades when women's friendships, along with the coffee klatch, have been trivialized and denigrated.

But I believe a sea of change in values and attitudes is coming in America. I believe we are witnessing the beginning of a grass-roots movement among women in churches and communities across America, affirming the importance of women's friendships—to the woman herself, to her family, to her nation. As my friend Linda LeSourd Lader reminded us in a speech to a women's group, "If mama ain't happy, ain't nobody happy." And there are lots of mamas, and single women, who know intuitively that they need richer, deeper relationships with their mothers, daughters, and friends for their psychological well-being. And there's a battalion of young women in this culture who desperately yearn for relationships with older women as mentors.

As a psychologist who works almost exclusively with women, I believe in the power of our female bonds to stave off loneliness, to help us flesh out an identity, and to encourage us in the time-honored task of nurturing the younger generation.

Finally, when I talk about clients in the following pages, I have been careful to provide a composite picture of the kinds of human needs and problems I encounter as a therapist. None of these examples are reflective of a specific client.

I care about women. And I have written this book to celebrate our female relationships by offering encouragement and practical help in deepening those bonds we hold dear.

1

• • •

The Necessary Company of Women

In addition to helping us grow and giving us

pleasure and providing aid and comfort,

our intimate friendships shield us from loneliness.

Judith Viorst, *Necessary Losses*

I grew up in the company of women.

After my father's untimely death when I was two, my beloved granddaddy was the only significant male who populated the landscape of my early childhood. I was surrounded by women in an extended family that included my mother, paternal grandmother, sister Sandy, assorted aunts, and female cousins.

But mostly I remember Granny. She was a tall, rawboned, southern farm woman who dropped out of school in the eighth grade. Intelligent, she read the local newspaper and her oversized black Bible daily. I can still see her sitting in an overstuffed chair in the afternoon light, her Bible open in her lap. Perpetually dressed in an apron, house dress, and stockings rolled in fat sausages around her ankles where they nestled in low-cut desert boots, Granny was an original.

She was the first people detective I ever knew. As I grew up, she often fixed her penetrating eyes on my soul and asked questions no one else ever dared: "How's life with your mother?" and "Do you miss your father?" Over the years, by her example, Granny taught me how to ask probing, open-ended questions. In a world where adults talked and seldom listened, she taught me that asking and listening meant caring.

My grandmother was always *there* when I needed her, and need her I did, since from the time I was two until I was five, she was my surrogate mother. Those were the years Mother took baby Sandy and went to another town to find work as a telephone operator. I had, in truth, lost two parents.

But I could always find Granny—either in the kitchen, where she reigned supreme, or in the garden, where her sun-drenched poke bonnet could be seen peeping through the ripening stalks of corn. Granny was an island of security to me. It was no small comfort to know I could always count on her for conversation or a piece of her delectable pie (she baked two daily). Until I went to live with my mother, Granny fed my hunger for love and taught me about intimacy and the necessary company of women.

From the depth of her own relationships with her mother and with Granddaddy, Granny taught me it was possible to be close to other people. An extrovert, she also taught me that women need the fellowship of other women or they wither. She was never happier than when she, Granddaddy, Sandy, and I piled into the old, black Ford on Sunday afternoons to go visiting. Sunday was the day she reconnected with her female friends, a time when she talked about her problems and her life.

From my vantage point in the back seat of the car, I understood intuitively that the love of a good man would never meet all of a woman's emotional needs, that women need the communion of other women to feel whole.

Women need other women

It sounds like a truism to say that women are relational beings who need the empathy, wisdom, and friendship of other women. From our earliest relationship with our mother, which shapes our personality, to our last great challenge, facing our own mortality, we look to the women in our lives to validate our feelings—to understand. If we have close emotional ties with our mothers, daughters, friends, and mentors—in addition to the men in our lives—our lives are richer, and our mental and physical health are better. On the other hand, if we are too often lonely and if we lack close female connections, we pay a high price emotionally—sometimes in depression, sometimes in anxiety, always in low self-esteem.

A national survey conducted by the Roper Organization on relationships of American women between the ages of seventeen and sixty reveals that "relationships seem to be the only reliable source of joy for many women."[1] For the women polled, having good relationships with husbands and children was crucial, ahead of money, career, and a good sex life.

In addition to good relationships with husbands and children, our relationships with other women are among our significant emotional bonds. While men provide the sense of *other* (as husbands and friends), women are *mirrors* for our femaleness our whole life long. From our symbiotic friendships of preadolescence to our friendships in old age, we look to other women to help us understand and shape our lives.

But we are not all equal in our ability to forge deep and lasting emotional bonds. Some of us are more capable of intimacy than others. While this may seem mysterious, our capacity for warm, loving relationships is traceable to our earliest emotional bonds with our parents, and particularly our mother. She is the first female we knew and loved. Or attempted to love.

The mother knot

Each of us begins life in the company of one woman who will have a deep and lasting effect upon our self-image, our capacity for intimacy as an adult, and our ability to nurture our children. Usually it is our biological mother or permanent mother substitute who profoundly influences our perceptions about ourselves, our lives, and our significant relationships. She is our first and primary attachment figure in early infancy.[2] While fathers are critical in our sex role development, discipline, and achievement, mother is the architect of intimacy for both sexes. By nurturing us, she gives us a legacy of mother love or mother woe that we pass on to the next generation. At her knee we learn to speak the language of the heart, or we first have our hearts broken.

From our mother, we learn to be comfortable with our own sex Through intimacy with her we learn it is safe to show our friends our hearts

We experience the reality of best friends, described by the ancients as "a second self," "a single soul dwelling in two bodies."[3]

But if we have been abused, rejected, or kept at bay by this woman whose love we desperately sought and needed? We may find it hard to trust other women with our vulnerable selves. We may also have difficulty relating to our daughters, with whom we closely identify. For it is from our mother that we learn how to nurture our daughters in positive, life-giving ways or that we receive a legacy of pain which we may unwittingly pass on to the next generation. From her we also learn to love ourselves, or we begin to absorb the message that we are unworthy of love.

The voices of women

In my years of working with young mothers through a national advocacy group and in my work as a psychotherapist, I have heard women speak of the *power* their relationship with their mother has in shaping their relationships with their daughters, sisters, friends, and even mentors. Over the years I have heard the joy, felt the longing, and witnessed the tears as women have spoken to me about their female bonds. Listen to some of their stories:

Twenty-two-year-old Sarah lives in an efficiency in downtown New York and pursues graduate studies in painting. Says Sarah, "My mother is a character. When we were sick as little kids, she'd take us on whirlwind shopping trips. We'd trudge behind her, clutching our brown paper bags to throw up in. While she may not have been June Cleaver, she was extremely loving and supportive. Now that I'm doing the starving artist thing, she is very encouraging. She believes in me and right now I need that."

Anna, who lives in Atlanta and is the mother of five children, currently struggles with depression. "I have never felt close to my mother," she says. "She was a single parent who was seldom home. By day she was an accountant; by night she was a student, taking classes to advance her career. When she was home, she was angry and verbally abusive—a house afire. Who could get close to that?"

Twenty-nine-year-old Miriam is close to her mother and best friends with her sister Jennifer. "Even though we live states apart and have crazy work and personal lives, we try to see each other once or twice a year. Jennifer will call up. 'Just say yes,' she'll command. After I've agreed, I usually find out I've committed to Cancun or Montreal. We're very different, but we have a first-rate friendship."

"I've just lost another friend," laments Marla, a thirty-year-old conference planner. "I know I'm too demanding, but I only realize this in hindsight. It's a vicious cycle. I have very few friends, so I count heavily on the few I do have. Too heavily. I've got to quit driving people away before I completely ruin my social life."

Gina, forty-two, has four children and a fifth en route. "I love children," she says beaming. "My mother had seven kids, but we all felt loved. Ever since I was small, I've wanted kids. Especially daughters. I love my two sons, but my daughters and I have a special kind of tie."

At forty-five, Lisa is locked in a struggle with her sixteen-year-old daughter. She wonders if her hostile relationship with an alcoholic mother is now being repeated in her relationship with her daughter. "I try to give my daughter more love, more time, more attention than my mother gave me. Some days I feel good about our relationship; other days, we're distant or hostile. And all those old feelings I had as a child—the loneliness and rejection—come rushing in."

Ginny, a thirtysomething new mother, hungers for a relationship with an older mother, a mentor. "All that I know about caring for my baby I'm having to learn from books," she laments. "My mother lives across the country, and we were never close to begin with. I need a mentor to teach me about marriage and rearing children."

We need women all our lives

Women always need other women to come alongside and speak their language: the language of the heart and of feelings. We shape each other's attitudes and self-definitions as we converse, and from each other we learn what it means to be female.

As preschoolers, we forge a sex role identity as we identify with our mother. Starting about age four, we begin to have same-sex friends and learn to take turns as we play. This is the beginning of learning about cooperation and fair play with peers—skills that will later translate into taking turns in our conversations. As adolescents we monitor our friends—the way they dress and relate to the opposite sex. And in adulthood we look for peers and mentors to teach us valuable skills, including how to be mothers and wives.

At each stage of development we need enough close friends or key players in our lives to share our confidences, stave off loneliness, and flesh out our self-definitions.

Two friends find a private table in the middle of a noisy, crowded restaurant. To passersby, these attractive women in their mid forties are simply talking. But to the women, something significant is happening. Ann confesses to Beth that she is having trouble with Tim, her husband, and is thinking about leaving him. Beth, a veteran of a twenty-year, solid-gold marriage, listens intently. Ann cries quietly and carefully wipes her cheeks with a napkin, trying not to smear her mascara. Gently, Beth empathizes with Ann's feelings, asks questions, and confesses that ten years earlier she, too, felt like leaving her husband. "Really?" says Ann. "I didn't know you and Mike had similar problems." Then Beth tells Ann about the help they got and the changes they've made in their relationship and how glad she is that she didn't leave him.

In time both women rise to go. Ann feels lighter, more hopeful. Her best friend understands and has been there before her. Moreover, she has suggested counseling before taking further action.

The women embrace and go to their separate cars, their separate lives. But a marriage has been helped, perhaps even saved, while two women were having lunch.

So what's the problem?

Many American women recognize their need for best friends or soul mates and make room in their lives for female camaraderie, but others find that cultural pressures and attitudes war against female friendships. By emphasizing heterosexual relationships above all else, our culture trivializes the importance of female friendships. In fact, sociologist Pat O'Connor states in *Friendships Between Women* that until the seventies the subject of women's friendships was largely ignored by writers and researchers alike.

There has been a tendency, says O'Connor, to view women's relationships with other women as "two-faced," "gossipy," or "a juvenile phase in the progression towards 'normal' heterosexual development."[4] The implication is that marriage meets all of women's emotional needs and, consequently, supplants the need for female friendships.

Another factor that makes it hard for some women to pursue friendships is their husbands' attitudes. One of my friends, a prominent Washingtonian, feels that "hard charging" men may be threatened by their wives' close female friendships. She says, "As a result, many of us engage in a conspiracy of silence. We don't talk about our two-hour lunches with our close friends. It's almost like it's our little secret."

In addition, many of us feel our female relationships suffer because of life in the fast track. Women in the nineties are living time-pressured lives and are often overwhelmed by the demands of family and career. Heidi Brennan, director of public policy for Mothers at Home, a national advocacy group, says, "Women today don't have time for friendships. We're more task oriented in the nineties, and friendship takes a lot of time." She adds, "People miss the backyard fence. Even working women. Women are community people, and even in the workplace, we attempt to create a sense of community."

One of my friends, a mother of two young sons whose career has recently skyrocketed, says, "It's much harder to see my friends now. For me to make time in my life for another woman, there has to be a payoff. She either has to be a very close friend or help me grapple with the issues I'm facing in my marriage or with my boys. I no longer have time for the small talk or the preliminaries of friendship."

A 1990 Gallup Mirror of America survey supports these observations, indicating that loneliness is on the rise in America. And loneliness sometimes comes with a high price tag. According to the *Fort Worth Star-Telegram* (October 27, 1993), Adele Gaboury lay dead in her home for four years before her neighbors thought to look inside. They just assumed the reclusive woman was in a nursing home. So Adele's thoughtful neighbors in Worcester, Massachusetts, notified the post office to stop delivering her mail after she hadn't been seen for two years, and called the utility company to shut off her water when frozen pipes burst one winter and water came spilling out under the door. Finally, the police found Adele's decaying body in the kitchen amid several feet of trash.

Adele had lived on her street for forty years.

Fortunately, most of us do not live such private, isolated lives. Yet our frequent moves and our divorces take their toll. We may have plenty of acquaintances, but what we tend to lose are our friends. The same Gallup survey also found that one out of four adults would like more friends, though half of those admit they don't have enough time to spend with their current friends. Women who work outside their homes, adults with children living at home, and the thirtysomething generation complain the most about lack of time for friendships.

If we have little or no discretionary time, we will have few, if any, deep friendships. It takes fallow, kick-back time to nurture relationships, and with the cultural emphasis on achievement in the workplace, friendships with other women are the first to go. One high-powered female executive was asked how she lived the superwoman life. She sighed and quietly replied, "I gave up my friends."

Not only do many women feel overwhelmed by all their caretaking tasks, but few of us have mothers or aunts down the block to help with the children or to nurture us. Relatives live hundreds or thousands of miles away. So while we struggle valiantly to care for friends and family, we do not feel cared for in kind. Increasingly in my work as a therapist and in my encounters with women outside my office, I find many women who have no one except their beleaguered husbands to meet their emotional needs and to nurture them. One twenty-nine-year-old client who was struggling with health problems and several young children fell apart one night. Sobbing, she said to her husband, "*I* need a mother. *I* need someone to take care of me."

In another era, an older woman—a neighbor, a friend at church, a relative—would have stepped in to fill this void. But today few women have cross-generational friendships. As a result, some find the boot camp of mothering an emptying, exhausting experience. When I was working with younger mothers through Home by Choice, Inc., I heard one question asked repeatedly, like a broken refrain: "Where are those older women I need to teach me about rearing children, marriage, and life?" I have also read hundreds of letters from women at home who some days feel lost, lonely, and alone. They are starved for relationships with peers and older women of the Wise Women Society. The following is a letter from a young professional who's come home to care for her children and struggles with life:

> I left my job in public relations recently to stay home with my sons, Brendan and Timothy, who are one and three, respectively. I did so because I felt I could not be an effective professional and mother at the same time. Not when my sons were very young.

> I'm writing to you because I'm struggling in suburbia now that I've made the decision to come home. I find I need emotional support on a daily basis, but get little except from my husband. I need friends who are also adjusting to life at home, and I wish I could find a wise, older woman to give me advice about child rearing, marriage, and structuring my time.

> I'm home by choice, but just now it's awfully lonely. I desperately need the support of other women. Where can I find the relationships I need?

> Friendless in Atlanta

Although she feels alone, this woman apparently represents a current trend. *Barron's*, in its March 21, 1994 issue, says a counter revolution is underway: women are flocking home from the workplace. For several years, plunging interest rates made it possible to fund a mortgage on a single paycheck. Among the women boomeranging home, the greatest number are twenty- to twenty-four-year-olds, members of Generation X. When *Barron's* asked why these particular women, most of whom had employed mothers, are coming home, many gave the following answer: "I don't want to go to work so that my daughter can go to day care—or so I can support a baby-sitter."

As women come home in record numbers, they will find, as the legion of mothers already at home have found, that they need friends and older mentors. And some will need to work through their emotionally distant or rejecting relationships with their mothers. The latter will come home in more ways than one.

Celebrating our female bonds

In a culture that for the past three decades has valued work and achievement above all else, we need to affirm the central role that female relationships play in our lives. As Sue Leach, teaching leader for Bible Study Fellowship in Seattle and a former social worker, says, "Today in America women need permission to pursue female relationships." I agree. We need to realize that time spent with our friends is not wasted time. We don't need to be achievement driven every minute of the day. Sometimes we need to be productive relationship builders. For it is as we share our struggles, laugh, and occasionally cry that we feel lifted. Understood. Renewed.

As a daughter, a mother of daughters, and a psychologist who works almost exclusively with adult women, I believe our female connections have enormous influence on our well-being and overall psychological functioning. Because our relationships with our mothers give us a legacy of love or woe, it is paramount that we work through any painful relationships with them so we do not unwittingly pass on our emotional insecurity to the next generation. As Dr. David Allen, chief of psychiatry at the Minirth-Meier/New Life Clinic, says, "We can't take someone to a place we've never been." Although many of us have secure, loving relationships with our mothers, sisters, and daughters, others do not. So while affirming secure bonds, I have tried in this book to bring understanding and hope to those in pain.

I have also written this book to challenge older women, those women of a certain age, to pass the torch to a younger generation of women, many of whom are starved for mentors. Mentoring not only strengthens younger families, but for those of us in midlife it adds vitality and meaning to our lives and helps ensure a rich old age.

Finally, I need to say at the outset of our journey together that I have not always felt comfortable in the company of women. Though Granny taught me that intimacy was possible, my mother taught me that intimacy hurt. For Mother, herself a motherless child, intimacy equaled loss and abandonment—a legacy she bequeathed to me. It was only in my forties that I dealt with this early and powerful relationship. And, after much hard work and no little healing, I have come to my present place in life where I am rich in friends, emotionally close to my husband and my daughters, and at peace with my mother and myself.

As I have grown more self-accepting, I have come to appreciate the great gifts women give each other. My friend Heidi Brennan summed it up when she said, "To like your sex, you have to like yourself."

I like myself and I like my sex. And in my profession, as well as in my life, I work with women to help them strengthen their female bonds.

So let's look at our female relationships together and examine the tremendous importance these emotional ties have in our lives.

Let's celebrate the company of women.

2

• • •

Mother: Our First Connection

Though Mom didn't give us a high standard of living,

she gave us a high standard of life.

It didn't matter how many rooms our little migrant house had.

What mattered was what went on in those rooms.

Linda Weber, *Mom, You're Incredible*

I n the July 1991 issue of *Welcome Home* magazine, Pauline Powell writes:

My mom is my hero. Now that I am a mother of two, I realize what it took to fill the job of mother and to do it well. The sacrifices my mother made and the love she gave me have not gone unnoticed.

My most precious memories are of my adolescent years. The average teenage girl is not the popular head cheerleader who has a date every weekend. I felt ordinary and lonely as other teenagers probably have felt. Some kids turn to drugs, gangs, or other escapes to find security, acceptance, and love. I was lucky. I had my mom. She was home, and she really cared and took time to listen. I still remember vividly the long conversations we had while we baked together in the kitchen or while I stretched across her bed as she sewed. We talked about premarital sex, the dangers of drugs and alcohol, crushes I had, and the loneliness I was experiencing. She took the time to help build my self-esteem, and I felt important.

By the time I was in high school, I had a good network of friends and an active social life, but I always kept a good relationship with my mom. We did not avoid all skirmishes, yet we managed to respect each other and our differing views. She gave me the inner strength I needed to stand up for what I believed in and to make difficult choices and decisions in college and afterward.

Now I am a mother of two, ages five and three. Even though I have chosen a similar way to raise my boys, it was the love and the freedom my mother gave me that allowed me to become the person and mother I am today.

She shares her experiences with me and encourages me when I feel unappreciated and drained as a mother. When I really feel "pitzy," as she fondly puts it, as if I'm not making a difference in my kids' lives, I remember how I felt growing up. Because I always knew my mother would be there for me, I felt loved, safe, and secure.

I pray I can give that sense of security to my own boys.

In these words Pauline Powell of Lewiston, Maine, describes the emotional security her mother gave her. Pauline's mother created a strong, invisible, many-stranded cord of love that not only binds her daughter to her today and continues to strengthen her but also influences the lives of Pauline's children as well.

The power of mother love

What is this thing called mother love that has inspired poets across the centuries and has generated three decades of detractors among radical feminists? What is it about the bond between a mother and her child that is at the same time so powerful and life enhancing and yet so threatening to some? And why is maternal love so foundational that some women spend much of their adult lives either basking in its richness or working to understand why their mothers couldn't love them?

It all begins before birth. Even before we are able to see our mother's face, we come to recognize her voice in the confines of the womb. The womb is, in fact, a cacophony of sound. Once a French obstetrician inserted a hydrophone into a woman's uterus as she was giving birth. What did he hear? "He heard a virtual orchestra of sounds: the mother's loud, thumping heartbeat, all sorts of whooshing and gurgling, the faint voices of the mother and her doctor talking, and in the background, the unmistakable strains of Beethoven's Fifth Symphony."[1]

We hear our mother's heartbeat in the womb. After birth, we begin to focus on her face. In fact, scientists have found that babies only one minute old will turn their heads 180 degrees to look at a picture of a human face—whether "real or sketched, in the flesh or on film, two- or three-dimensional, even a mask with two eye-like dots."[2] But in time, not just any face will do. We soon prefer our mother's above all the rest. As for voices, studies show that while newborns love the sound of human voices, they love mother's best.

We were born, then, programmed to fall in love with our mother. As babies we resonated to her smile; we picked up on her moods; we talked to her with our coos. If we were fortunate, she listened, held us close, cooed back, and established eye contact again and again. A lovely duet between a mother and her baby began.

Dr. David Allen believes that just as the womb provides a nurturing or holding environment for the baby, so the mother/child relationship is a nurturing environment. "The mother provides the child," says Dr. Allen, "with stability, consistency, predictability. That's what love is, providing a container or holding environment."

At birth, we began to fall in love with our mother, and if we were lucky, she was able to fall in love with us as well. If we were among those most fortunate of women, our mother had enough love in her maternal well to nurture us. She gave us what child development experts agree all babies need whether they are born in poverty or wealth—"sensitive, consistent, responsive" mothering. She didn't have to be a nurse, a doctor, or a psychologist to give us what we required for our emotional development. She just needed to be a reasonably whole being able to devote herself to the demanding tasks of caring for an infant. She needed, in the words of the famous pediatrician Donald W. Winnicott, to be able to give us "good enough mothering."

A first lesson in trust

As we related to our mother in those earliest months, we understood the gist of what she said to us, long before we knew the meaning of her words. We picked up on the emotional inflections in her voice. We recorded the essential emotional meaning of all she said, and we stored this awareness in our primitive brain.[3]

According to psychologist Evelyn Thoman, we possess a highly developed limbic brain system at birth that has its own intelligence and memory. It is the seat of all our emotions. Although the limbic system is preverbal, it records persistent feelings, whether happy and secure or sad and anxious. "Adults often talk of feelings that well up for no apparent reason and seem unrelated to the logical realities at hand," write Thoman and Browder. "The complaint 'I've done so well—why do I feel so bad?' has become the lament of many a high wattage baby boomer."[4] If we had primarily sad and insecure feelings as babies, we develop "a vague, illogical, ineffable feeling of being disjointed with the world."[5]

Feeding, touching, and cuddling are necessary and powerful aspects of mother love. As babies, we needed to be fed, held, and cuddled by our mother. As we grew, we needed to be able to go to her for comfort whenever we were afraid, lonely, sick, or distressed.

If we could, we learned to trust. And learning to trust our mother is the central task of infancy, according to psychoanalyst Erik Erikson. "Babies," he says, "are sensitive and vulnerable too."[6] Without trust, psychologist William Damon believes "there is little hope that an infant can feel the confidence in the self necessary to establish individuality and autonomy."[7]

How does trusting our mother affect our later emotional development? If we learned to trust her, we are able to trust our friends, husbands, and ourselves later on. But if we weren't able to trust her—if she proved physically and emotionally unavailable and undependable—we were bereft indeed. We learned as babies that life is a struggle and fear is the name of the game.

The power of this struck me when I was a graduate student doing research on the mother/baby attachment relationship. I spent three days at the University of Virginia watching videotapes of the Strange Situation, a laboratory experiment that allows psychologists to measure the attachment relationship that twelve- to eighteen-month-old children have with their mother or father. I was amazed. Some mothers after brief separations (they were waiting just outside in the hall) sailed back into the room, scooped up their sons or daughters, and comforted them beautifully. Soon their babies were happily engrossed in toys and other things. But other mothers were out of sync with their babies and were unable to comfort them. Some babies cried uncontrollably, no matter how much their mothers tried to soothe and caress them. Others were detached and avoided their mothers altogether.

At the end of those three days, I was an emotional wreck. Not only was I unnerved by all the crying I had heard, but the realization really hit me: as early as twelve months of age we know if we can trust our mother to respond to us! And even in infancy, we bask in this realization, or we develop ways of coping with our fear and anxiety.

And if we learn our mothers are trustworthy and reliable? We develop a capacity to move forward developmentally, taking essential risks, because of the undergirding power of our mother's love.

And if we are "let down"? If our mothers are rejecting, abusive, physically absent, or emotionally absent too long? We feel anxious, resulting from the trauma of being "dropped" and "falling forever," and we create defenses to protect our vulnerable selves.[8] Defenses that may be hard to dismantle later on.

Diane Bengson describes this need to be held in *Discovering Motherhood*: "My baby wanted to be held almost constantly, and he let me know in no uncertain terms. I loved the feel of his skin and the wonderful smell of his neck just below his velvety soft earlobes. When he relaxed, his body seemed to fit mine just like a puzzle piece. But I was quite unprepared to share my body so completely with another person and to rearrange the ways I did almost everything, from spreading jam on my toast (one handed) to brushing my teeth."[9]

Fortunately, Diane was able to adjust and accommodate her baby's need to be held, and when her son reached a year old, the holding time greatly diminished. Her secure little boy was off and running, discovering his fascinating, safe world of home.

I have a friend, Cecelia, whose second child, Janine, also required almost constant holding as an infant, and when she didn't get it, Janine sobbed. Exhausted, Cecelia consulted her pediatrician. What was she to do? Wisely, the doctor gently encouraged her by saying that if she could just persevere and satisfy her daughter's emotional neediness, in time the girl would become emotionally secure. As she grew, she would become independent and need her mother less. Cecelia persevered, and today Janine is a bright, secure five-year-old who is healthily independent.

But not all of us were warmly and securely held by our mothers. Gina just learned recently that her mother did not hold her when she was a baby. "Instead, she used a little stuffed animal with a place to insert a baby bottle." Gina wonders if this early experience and the fact that neither parent cuddled her are related to her chronic depression. "I have felt almost no need to bond with anyone," she says. "I seem to be popular. I'm a leader and very independent. Although at forty-seven I have never married, I love to hug kids and animals."

The power of the mother's love and presence can hardly be overstated. For in that first year, but particularly between six and twelve months of age, we forged an attachment first to her and then to our father that has shaped our self-esteem, feelings of personal power, capacity for intimacy, and expectations about how others will respond to us.[10]

Writing in 1940, Sigmund Freud made a famous pronouncement when he described the child's relationship with his mother as "unique, without parallel, established unalterably for a whole lifetime as the first and strongest love object and as the prototype of all later love relationships for both sexes."[11]

The late British psychiatrist John Bowlby agreed. In a report to the World Health Organization, Bowlby said, "What is believed to be essential for mental health is that the infant or young child should experience a warm, intimate and continuous relationship with his mother (or permanent mother substitute) in which both find satisfaction and enjoyment."[12] Bowlby also believed that our relationship with our mother is the "foundation stone of personality."[13]

What about fathers?

If a mother's love is so critical to personality development, what about the power of a father's love? Obviously children need their father's love, time, and attention as well. Babies establish relationships with both parents which are distinct and different. Contrary to popular opinion, children need both.

In our attempts to erase gender differences in America in the past three decades, we have tried to make mothers and fathers interchangeable. In fact, to say that mothers and fathers have different gifts and provide their children with different parenting styles is politically incorrect heresy.

This was illustrated recently when a friend flew to Los Angeles to defend motherhood on a national talk show. At one point the host asked my friend, "Can't dads nurture kids as well as moms?" When Kristie pointed out that anthropological evidence shows cross-culturally that mothers are paramount in infancy and dads are central in introducing children to the larger world, the audience went wild, hissing and booing loudly.

The audience was simply uninformed. Kristie, who had done her homework, was right. Psychologists have found, cross-culturally, that mothers relate to children through caretaking and nurturing while fathers forge an attachment through play.[14] Moreover, around the world dads spend less time interacting with babies than moms. Even in the kibbutz, where both parents are employed full-time and children are cared for by professional caretakers, kibbutz mothers are "more likely to vocalize, laugh, display affection, hold and engage in caregiving than fathers."[15] One Swedish study found that even when dads stayed home with the kids and moms worked full-time, the mothers still spent more time holding the children and giving them affection than did the fathers.[16]

But our father is critically important in helping our mother care for us and in creating warm, strong attachments to us from infancy on. Dr. David

Allen, who says the mother/child relationship provides his model for psychotherapy, believes the role of the father is to encircle, protect, contain the mother/child relationship. "The father provides a nurturing environment for both mother and child," says Allen, "and when fathers fail to do this, then societal trauma goes right to the child and it can destroy him."

We need our father, then, to love and support our mother. And we need him to relate to us as young girls and women. For daughters, father love was, and is, a potent psychological force in shaping our sense of competency and confidence. If, as little girls, we were adored by our father, today we are more likely to be comfortable with men and supremely confident. And if our father loved our mother, applauded her mothering, and encouraged us to develop our gifts, we will tend to feel competent as women, without being driven. When we, in turn, become mothers, we can devote ourselves to motherhood and our children for a season without feeling we must constantly achieve. After all, we have already captured our father's heart, and so we do not have to identify with him so strongly that we forgo our mothering feelings.

Father love is just as critical as mother love in personality development. Our relationships with both parents, in effect, merge in adulthood to give us a generalized sense of worthiness or worthlessness. Both are important. Each is distinct.

Why do our beginnings matter?

You may ask why all the emphasis on our beginnings? After all, we can't remember our earliest months and years, so what's the point?

The point is, as infants, we developed different patterns of attachment. Basically, we developed feelings of emotional security or insecurity in our closest relationships—our relationships with our parents. As very young children, we formed inner working models of ourselves and our world— patterns of attachment—based on the way our parents treated us. Although these models operated outside of our conscious awareness, they influenced our perceptions nevertheless.[17] And psychologists have found that patterns of attachment, once established, tend to persist.

Psychologist Mary Ainsworth and her colleagues found that in the early years, but particularly in the first six to twelve months, babies develop three patterns of attachment.

If a mother comes when her baby cries, and if she picks up on the child's signals and responds lovingly, then the baby tends to become *securely attached* to her. The child learns early on that mother can be counted on to meet her physical and emotional needs sensitively.[18] As the child grows, her self-esteem soars, and she learns to expect others to treat her as her mother and father did. If a child feels emotionally secure, even as a pre-schooler and kindergartner, she is likely to be popular with her peers, cooperative with adults, and better able to explore her world than her insecure counterparts.[19]

If, on the other hand, a mother is unpredictable—if she sometimes responds lovingly, sometimes not, so that her child is never able to count on her love—then the child may develop an *anxious-resistant* attachment to her. Babies who forge an anxious-resistant relationship with their mothers are often angry, clinging, and inconsolable after brief separations from them. They may also develop this pattern of attachment if their parents try to control them by threats of abandonment.[20] And if babies forge an anxious-resistant attachment to their mothers, they may be anxious and clinging in their love relationships thereafter.

Finally, some mothers reject their children. When this happens in infancy, babies learn to avoid their mothers and develop an *anxious-avoidant* relationship.[21] Even in infancy, these babies learn that intimacy equals rejection and hurt. On the surface, children with anxious-avoidant attachment relationships appear to be independent. But avoiding a primary attachment is a defense mechanism, a way of warding off further emotional pain.[22]

As children grow, these attachment patterns persist. For example, one study found that six-year-olds who were classified as *securely attached* were intimate, relaxed, and friendly around their parents. Those who were *anxious-resistant* were sad, fearful, sometimes hostile, and sometimes close. Those classified as *anxious-avoidant* kept their parents at a distance and were politely impersonal.[23]

Some of us may remember feeling rejected by our mothers as small children and may still struggle with the feeling that we were denied good enough mothering. Even now we may have little confidence that we will receive care, comfort, and understanding from our mothers or from others, for that matter. Instead, we expect to be rebuffed. We are those women who "try to live without the love and support of others."[24]

But that's hard to do. So we develop ways of providing some of the love and attention we need. We may become compulsive caregivers, giving love and attention to others in order to glean some for ourselves. Or we may flee intimacy because we fear rejection too much. Or we may become enmeshed in our romantic relationships, clinging tightly to boyfriends or husbands as we once did to our unpredictable mothers.

I often ask women, "Who comforted you as a child?" The answer is invariably revealing. If the answer is "my mother," the woman usually has warm and positive feelings for her mother. If she responds "both parents," then she was fortunate in having two warm, nurturing parents. If she says "no one," then I understand she is compulsively self-reliant—aloof and fiercely independent—because no one took care of her emotional needs. And if she says she doesn't remember, that too is significant. It may be that she has repressed childhood memories which are simply too painful to bring out to public view.

So our earliest relationships with our parents do matter. These emotional bonds influence our self-esteem as well as our capacity to forge intimate bonds with our husbands and with our children. And our bond with our mother also affects our relationships with other women: our peers, daughters, mentors. Said one woman who wasn't emotionally close to her alcoholic mother, "It was not until my twenties that I became comfortable in the presence of other women."

Mother: the mirror

In addition to the *quality* of our relationship with our mother, the fact that we are both female has greatly influenced our development. In 1977 Nancy Friday wrote a blockbuster book entitled *My Mother/Myself,* which touched a nerve for thousands of American women. Friday suggested that a daughter's identity was inextricably bound up in her relationship with her mother. "When a mother holds her child in her arms, whether it is her son or her daughter, she feels many emotions. When that child is the same sex as she, she *sees* herself. She feels a tidal wave of every emotion she has ever felt—love, fear, anxiety and hate. It is not so much what a mother wants for her daughter that will determine how far a girl will go. More than anything, it is the mother's own self-esteem that will influence the daughter's emotional separation and independence."[25]

Shared gender also means that daughters do not separate and individuate as much as sons, says researcher Nancy Chodorow.[26] Sons pull away from their mothers at an early age and begin to identify with their fathers. According to psychologist Ruthellen Josselson, a daughter identifies with the first person she loves. "Attachment implies sameness. 'I love my mother and want to grow up to be just like her' is the hallmark of the identification processes in the little girl. With becoming like mother and therefore pleasing her comes the assurance of remaining forever attached to her."[27] It is those shared personality characteristics with our mothers that help us form our personalities. Our relationship gives us a sense of self. By using our mother as mirror, we know what it is to be female.

Friends tell my daughters that they share some of my mannerisms and we all smile alike. A relative told Holly at a family reunion, "You look just like your mother did at your age, only you're better looking." Not only do my daughters share some of my physical traits—Holly acknowledges she is the third generation of Morrison women with flat feet—but each shares some of my interests. Kris majored in psychology, while Holly is a fine writer and editor. Each, though very much herself, has identified to some extent with me.

Of course, identification is easier when we are emotionally close to our mothers. Then we want to grow up to be like them in important ways. What happens when we are not? This can cause great ambivalence for the daughter. She may focus on her mother's faults and seek an identity that is wholly different. But she pays a high price psychologically if she fails to integrate something of her mother into her concept of self (her "domesticity, nurturance, dress or values"[28]). She may experience what psychologists call "identity diffusion," which means we are uncertain what it means to be female and we thus reject a part of ourselves. Writes Josselson, "Some aspect of mother must be mixed in the identity in order to bind it, to make it cohere."[29]

We not only need to be emotionally close to our mothers in childhood, but we need to stay close as adults. In her study of female identity, Ruthellen Josselson found that 85 percent of the women in her study remained close to their mothers in adulthood with "nearly half choosing her as the person they feel closest too or second closest to in all the world."[30] Interestingly, only 48 percent remained close to their fathers, and only two women said their fathers were closest or second closest to them. Josselson also found that many of the women she studied telephoned their mothers daily and asked for their advice. Most reported that their mothers gave them emotional support and practical help.

Josselson's findings are similar to those in a 1993 *New Woman* survey, particularly for single women. When asked to name the one person who loved them most and knew them intimately, single women invariably named their mothers. (Married women selected their husbands, and the divorced and widowed named their grown children.)[31] Said Jennifer, a twenty-eight-year-old, single woman from Wyoming, "My mother and I have a tremendous amount of respect for each other's judgment and we're very compatible. It's easy for us to spend time together. When I was sixteen, we traveled for a month in Europe and we had so much fun. Now we shop for clothes together and talk about things we've read. My mom has done so much for me I could never begin to pay her back."[32]

If a girl's relationship to her mother is secure and strong, she grows up feeling she can control the good things of her life. She calls; her mother comes. She is hurt; her mother speaks soothing words of comfort. She gets an award at school, and her mother dances around the kitchen, holding her daughter's hands. A daughter then develops a sense of personal efficacy and power.

"I remember as a small child the sense of power I felt with my mother," says Sabrina, a twenty-seven-year-old consultant. "I used to play a little song on my xylophone. 'I love my Mommy. I love my Mommy.' And my mother would come from any corner of the house, scoop me up, and plant a wet kiss on my cheek.

"When I went to college, I still called, this time by telephone, and we developed a wonderful friendship. Once when I was sick and had a high fever and stiff neck, Mom drove several hours immediately after she got off the phone to bring me home and care for me.

"It gives me an incredible sense of security knowing that as long as my mother lives, as long as she has her health, she will come when I call. What does that allow me to do? I can make decisions. I can take risks. Best of all, I can trust others, God, life. My mom taught me to enjoy life—the moment—and believe that good things will come to me."

"Children learn early in life," said Bowlby, addressing the American Psychiatric Association in 1986, "that life is either a gift to be enjoyed or a burden to be borne." As a psychologist, I believe that our mothers instill this in us.

Linda Weber begins her book *Mom, You're Incredible* with a tribute to her mother who had the daunting task of rearing three children in impoverished circumstances. Her abusive father abandoned the family, leaving her mother to support three children on two hundred dollars a month.

We lived in an apple orchard in a small structure built to house migrant workers. A couch sat against one wall of our tiny living room, and an old upright piano covered the opposite wall. If I stood in the center of the room, I could reach out and touch both pieces at the same time.

Cold floors. No carpet. An oil stove for heat. The rent was $25 a month. We used spare apple boxes for cupboards and dressers and covered them with old tea towels. We were allowed to collect the fallen apples and added to them the wild asparagus that grew here and there among the trees.

When the school year began, if we kids were lucky, we'd get to choose one pair of shoes to last us the year. Naturally our wardrobe selection left more than a little to be desired. Most of our clothes were hand-me-downs from other families.... When I got to high school, a friend's mother made clothes for me so that I could look like everyone else.[33]

Sounds pretty bleak, right? Yet Linda's mother loved her children and gave them the sense that they were worthy. She focused on "the heart and the spirit" and raised resilient children, among them a daughter who clearly feels that she had an "incredible mom."

The mother connection. A mother lode of intimacy or pain. A sense of belonging to others and to ourselves. When we have experienced the power of mother love, we not only have higher self-esteem and a greater capacity for trust and intimacy than those who have not, but we also have a different life experience than those who were, and continue to be, maternally deprived.

But the maternally deprived can take heart. They too can find healing and grace. I know. It happened to me. Those of us who lack that positive mother connection can find other sources of love and acceptance. As we shall see, we also can find a way home.

3

• • •

Mother Love

Happy families are all alike;

every unhappy family is unhappy in its own way.

Leo Tolstoy, *Anna Karenina*

Carla Risener Bresnahan, a mother of three children who works evenings as a mental health counselor, captures the essence of the secure mother/daughter bond in a piece she wrote originally for the May 1993 issue of *Welcome Home.*

When I was a child, my mother's lap was the warmest and safest place in the world. On my mother's lap, all the troubles of childhood would fade away, and I would be perfectly secure and content.

I remember simply sitting on her lap for long periods of time. I suspect she had dishes to do, clothes to wash, errands to run, and yet, I sat. But I do not recall her ever telling me she had something to tend to. In fact, it was always I who ventured off first. Perhaps I had finally awakened from sleep, or my childhood hurts had been comforted away, but when I was emotionally full, I got up.

My mother had two children younger than I, so how was she able to provide this precious gift of time? I wondered this yesterday, when my own two-year-old daughter, still drowsy from nap time, curled up on my lap. I stroked her hair softly, sang sweet lullabies, and eventually, when she was ready to face the world, she got up.

I, too, had dishes and laundry to do, errands to run and (not to mention) a baby to feed. But my memories of childhood tugged at my heart. I was so happy with myself that I had allowed my need for perfection to slip for a while. Only then did I realize how my own mother managed that special lap time. She, too, had allowed chores to wait.

I also realized my mother had given me two precious gifts, one to her daughter the child, the other to her daughter the adult. To the child, she gave comfort, love, security, and intimacy. To the adult, she modeled a valuable lesson: that a mother's lap is a child's sanctuary.

Thanks, Mom; I needed both.

For Carla, the lap was a symbol of her mother's warmth and emotional accessibility. In her mother's lap Carla felt secure, and only when she was "emotionally full," did she run off to play. Her sensitive mother allowed her to determine when her deepest needs had been met. And today as Carla mothers her own children, she gives them the gifts her mother gave her.

I am reminded of another "lap" story told to me by a single friend who has a close relationship with her nephew John. Recently Karen had three-year-old John stay with her at her apartment in Little Rock for a weekend. She says, "John just sat on my lap in the dark looking out the window at the stars and the city lights below. We sat for so long I thought little John was asleep. He was utterly still and quiet, but when I looked carefully, I found he was wide awake, just basking in the experience. We must have sat there, ever so still, for hours."

Women who had an available maternal lap during childhood probably had a strong connection with their mothers. This connection has given them a leg up all their lives. University of Massachusetts pyschologist Seymour Epstein found in his research that when women experience maternal love and acceptance in childhood they develop "a sense of love worthiness" as adults.[1] This sense of love worthiness, in turn, produces high self-esteem. When a woman possesses high self-esteem, says Epstein, she has internalized a loving parent who is proud of her successes and accepting of her failures. The woman with low self-esteem, on the other hand, carries inside her a harsh parent who is devastatingly critical of her failures.[2]

And this positive legacy gets passed on. In fact, psychologist Margaret Ricks found that a woman's positive memories of being accepted by her mother are the strongest predictor of how secure her own children will feel in her love. That is, women who felt secure in their mother's love are more likely to have secure infants themselves.[3]

When a woman from Voice of America came to interview me several weeks ago, we sat on the couch talking. She, seven months pregnant with her third child, plans to give up her job to stay home with her children. As we talked about her life, she mentioned that she loved spending time with her seventy-year-old mother. "She's wonderful," she said. "I don't know how she raised us six kids as well as she did. Now that I have my own, I think she has so much to teach me. I just want to enjoy her as much as I can." Kathy is typical of women I talk to who feel secure in their mother's love.

Mother as friend

All of the women I interviewed who said they were emotionally close to their mothers growing up regarded them as trusted and valued friends in adulthood. These daughters were able to make the transition from the dependent parent/child relationship of earlier years to a peer-based friendship. Charmaine, a thirty-two-year-old, former Washington, D.C. policy analyst, says, "After my husband, Mom is still the first person I turn to for shopping excursions and advice. I probably have fewer female friends because my mom and I spend so much time together. We are very much alike, and we feel comfortable together."

Mary, an eighty-eight-year-old retired secretary, remembers that as a child she took her attentive mother for granted. "I didn't realize until I was older what a wonderful, caring, and devoted mother she was. Our relationship was always close, but after I became an adult we were much closer emotionally. I adored her. I have many wonderful, heartfelt memories of the life we had together for seventy-three years."

Mother as confidante

When we have a secure relationship with our mother, not only does she become a friend in adulthood, but she is entrusted with important secrets. With this lifetime friend we can share our feelings without fear of betrayal or reprisal. Janet, a thirty-six-year-old banker, says, "My mother and I have always been extremely close. As a child I felt safe to confide in her and continue to do so today. She is not only my mom, but she is also my best friend."

Mother as cheerleader

Mother has seen us at our weakest and will do so again. She knows our dreams and encourages us to pursue them. "My mother is the most affirming person I know, so she really holds me up and keeps me going when I am unsure of myself," says Leslie, a thirty-year-old graphics designer. Mary Ellen, a thirty-four-year-old mother at home, says, "My mother comforted me through difficult times in adolescence and was my greatest source of emotional support and self-esteem."

Women who feel secure in their adult relationships with their mothers report that their moms applaud their achievements while fulfilling their own potential. This cheerleader mom does not live through her daughter's successes (she has her own fulfilling life), but she is affirming and supportive.

Mother as role model

Mothers are also important role models, particularly for emotionally secure women. Whereas daughters who are estranged from their mothers often reject their mothers' values and lifestyle, secure daughters look to their mothers to help them chart their course.

Charmaine says her mother has long been an inspiration to her personally and professionally. "I saw her tough it out to get her Ph.D. when I was a child," says Charmaine. And that means a lot to Charmaine today as she works part-time on her doctorate at the University of Virginia while nurturing baby Hannah.

Diana, a thirty-two-year-old psychotherapist at the Minirth-Meier/New Life Clinic in Northern Virginia, admires her mother as her mentor. She remembers fondly those days when her mother, an executive in the garment district of New York City, took her as a child to her office. "She was a career woman who made her work look challenging, fun, and satisfying."

Beyond serving as role models at home and at work, mothers provide living character studies as well. Charmaine witnessed her mother care for a bedridden mother-in-law for two years before her death. This was significant not only because the parents ensconced Charmaine's grandmother in their living room, providing around-the-clock care, but because Charmaine's mother was not emotionally close to her mother-in-law. Charmaine was impressed that her mother did the right thing for the older woman, despite her lack of warm feelings.

Mother as secure base and nurturer

Not only was our mother our "secure base" when we were children, providing the freedom to explore our world,[4] but she remains bound to us by an invisible tether as we mature. If the relationship is close, we remember those feelings of warmth and security we had as children while we are making our own mark on the world.

Megan Beyer, the wife of Virginia's lieutenant governor, grew up in a large Catholic household with five siblings. Her father was a doctor and her mother, says Megan unabashedly, was Donna Reed. "My mother gave me an incredible sense of emotional security. Each night she'd tuck all of us into bed. When I came home from school, she was there most days. I remember having a sinking feeling on those rare days when she was absent. I always wanted her to be home. I felt more secure knowing she was there." Megan, who has elected to work in the media part-time, is drawing on this legacy of good mothering to nurture her small daughter.

Chris, an office manager of a mental health center, describes her childhood relationship with her mother as "close, comforting, and nurturing." Chris drew on this relationship when her own daughter was killed at twenty-one in a car accident. Now Chris speaks frequently to women's groups, offering comfort to other mothers who have also lost children. She says, "When my daughter died, I really needed my mother, and she came through for me. I value and treasure our relationship."

When we become mothers ourselves

Even when we have a secure attachment to our mother, this relationship deepens once we become mothers ourselves. In our twenties and thirties we may distance ourselves from our mother as we work to establish a measure of psychological independence. But when our first baby is born, we suddenly find ourselves preoccupied with our mother. How did she handle colic? Diaper rash? Teething? We need her counsel; most of all, we need her presence. We find our mother becomes an even closer friend as we now have something powerful in common: our love for this wonderful new baby.

Heather, a former C.P.A., says her earlier relationship with her mom was "very close but not without its ups and downs." However, "as an adult, my relationship with her has developed into a deep-rooted friendship." Now a mother at home herself, Heather adds, "My appreciation and respect for her effort and commitment in her mothering role have really come about since I have had children."

Pam, a forty-year-old free-lance writer and editor, believes that as her children grow and negotiate different stages of development, she becomes more understanding and appreciative of her mom. "I have always felt comfortable asking my mom questions, and we've been able to discuss anything. Sometimes I can even predict when my mom, who lives hundreds of miles away, will call. I can just feel it. I pick up the phone and sure enough, it's her."

Living our mother's dream

When we are close to our mother and identify strongly with her, we may discover, to our surprise, that we are living her dream. Carlie, a former tax attorney and partner at a prestigious law firm, says that although her mother was a fifties woman, Carlie has become just like her. "My journey into motherhood has brought me full circle," she admits.

Carlie's mother, a college-educated junior executive for a major department store, left her job to care for her children because she felt staying home to care for them was her "destiny." "She felt no guilt whatsoever," says Carlie, "or that she had given up anything important to take care of us."

Before her first son, Peter, was born when she was thirty-five, Carlie thought that full-time motherhood was just one of many choices she could make. But her attitudes have since changed. "Now that I have three sons and have stayed home for nearly seven years I, like my mother, view child rearing not just as a choice but as my destiny."

Megan also feels she, in some respects, is living her mother's dream. Megan's mother clipped newspaper articles on current events and posted them on the refrigerator for her six children to read. As an adult, Megan became a TV journalist and today works part-time while she cares for twenty-one-month-old Clara. Like her mother, Megan has managed to marry her love of current events with her desire to raise a family.

Dru Ramey, who runs the San Francisco Bar Association, has also strongly identified with her mother, Stell Ramey, a medical school professor. Dru says of her mother, "Her success was the result of her mother's dream and her own hard work." Dru's grandmother, an illiterate Jew from Alsace-Lorraine, worked in a sweatshop when Stell was growing up, and she urged her daughter to acquire an education. At seventy-six, Stell is professor emeritus from Georgetown University and, according to Dru, earns more money giving speeches than her daughter earns working full-time as a lawyer. "I am incredibly proud of her," admits Dru.

The gift of intimacy

A further gift that comes from a secure relationship with our mother is the gift of intimacy—a gift we share with our husbands, children, and close friends. Having been close to our mother since infancy, we do not erect walls for others to scale, as do our insecure counterparts. Nor do we engage in push-pull behavior. Instead, intimacy feels natural, so natural we may take it for granted.

In my conversations with women who report close bonds with their parents, especially their mother, I find they are quite nonchalant about this whole subject of intimacy. It's as if I'm asking about something they do well and just don't think about. After all, why concern oneself with something one already possesses? "Of course I know how to be intimate," said one woman, laughing. "I just don't go around talking about it. Like people who are sexually satisfied don't go around endlessly talking about sex."

My friend Anne Marie McMichael says she has only recently learned to consciously label and appreciate the gifts her mother gave her, particularly the gift of intimacy. Anne Marie says, "I always had a hard time waking up as a child. So my mother would come into my room each morning with a warm cup of milk laced with coffee and a piece of toast and gently awaken me. She would then sit down and talk to me for a few minutes. She did this throughout my years at home.

"In high school my friends would drive me home, and as I walked up the sidewalk I could hear my mother playing the piano. I remember feeling quite happy that she would be home to hear me talk about my day.

"Mom was a great communicator. She talked openly about sex. I knew there was this *thing* between her and my father. They really loved each other and were sexually attracted to each other. Once when an uncle criticized her for her less-than-squeaky-clean house, she told me conspiratorially, 'It's not a clean house that brings your father home.' Because of what my mother gave me, I can nurture my children, husband, and friends."

As Anne Marie's story shows, a mother's capacity to be emotionally close to her daughter is no small thing. From this secure attachment flows the ability to trust others and to provide a safe place for our children, to pass on a bedrock sense of emotional security, while training them to speak the language of the heart. The daughter who has a loving and secure connection with her mother carries her high self-esteem, her ability to take risks, her inner confidence well. She goes through life knowing she has had a champion since birth—someone who has always been there to hear her out, lift her up, and cheer her on.

And what a world of difference that makes.

Heidi's Story

I can clearly remember sitting on the edge of my bed holding my new baby. We had just gotten home from the hospital, and my husband had left to pick up my mother at the airport. I had a tremendous need for her—not just because I suddenly felt helpless. I was ready to complete a psychological task. By becoming a mother, I needed to merge my life with hers in a new way. I was beginning to conduct my motherhood symphony, and I needed my composer to reassure me and remind me in case I forgot the music.

My life as a mother often seems like a continuous, special thread handed to me by my mother, and from her mother before. I am very close to my mom, but much of what I experience as our warm, emotional intimacy and easy rapport is not usually visible to others. We live on opposite sides of the country, exchanging phone calls every two weeks. Yet I continue to have a daily relationship with her through the memories of my childhood.

These memories are the foundation for how I nurture my children, reflecting my mother in so many things I do with them. I enjoy listening to classical music, especially ballet. As my own children spin around to the *Nutcracker Suite,* I recall my mother leaping and spinning through our living room, drawing me into her dance and joy of life. At times I am almost overcome with emotion just thinking about those moments. I feel tremendous peace within me as I spend time with my children in these memory-repeating ways.

My children love it when I turn their stuffed toys into puppets, speaking to them in funny voices. As I do this, I can hear my mother's vocal intonations and sense of humor in my own voice. Instantly, I feel a rapport with her, uninterrupted by time or distance.

Motherhood was not just an opportunity for my mother's creative expression—it was a creative experience in and of itself. She would spontaneously sit down with crayons and paper to draw pictures with me. She was not so much teaching me to draw, but relating to me through that medium—and, in that process, teaching me to love and express myself freely.

My mother could not afford to buy me lessons in dance, drama, art, and other such unique opportunities. Instead, she nurtured me and my siblings in her own artistic ways. Dance, drama, and art were some of the media she used for communicating her love to us and in creating emotional security within us.

While parents today seem to worry about giving their children enough outlets to help them build self-esteem, the personal lessons I draw from my mother's gifts to me accent what I believe my children need most—the daily creation of spiritual and emotional avenues for communication between us. It is through these that I teach my children. This is not primarily a didactic method with measurable outcomes—the things we tend to assume most about education. Instead, I try to follow my children's development with empathy, encouragement, and joy through the most mundane of life's daily experiences.

As I do, my mother's presence is not just close by, it is inside me.

Heidi Brennan is the public policy director for Mothers at Home, a national advocacy group, and the mother of four children, whom she is homeschooling. She has appeared on radio and television to share her love of mothering.

4

• • •

Mother Woe

Happy children do not ask why their mothers or anybody else love them; they merely accept it as a fact of existence. It is those who have received less than their early due of love who are surprised that anyone should be fond of them, and who seek for explanation of the love that more fortunate children take for granted.

Anthony Storr, British psychoanalyst

Eight o'clock in the morning. The first client of the day has arrived. She is a woman in her thirties, exquisitely dressed. She is still except for her hands: they keep twisting and retwisting a crumpled Kleenex. This woman is scared: she is struggling to understand why she has such a difficult time with her intimate relationships and why she cannot connect emotionally with her aloof and distant husband or preteen daughters. She longs for intimacy, but it continues to elude her.

As I listen, I ask her about her relationship with her mother.

"Mom was home, but she was always preoccupied. She seldom asked me about my feelings, and I knew as a child she was unhappy. I guess she was depressed."

"Where did you go for comfort?" I ask.

"I didn't go to anyone," she replies. "I could only rely on myself. I became independent, self-sufficient."

These comments trigger a buzzer in my therapist brain. I believe this woman's current difficulties with her closest relationships may, in large measure, result from her failure to be securely attached to her mother as a child.

The emotionally disconnected

Writer and educator Elaine McEwan writes in *My Mother, My Daughter* that she was estranged from her mother for most of her adult life. She says, "I've never really been able to figure out how my mother and I were connected."[1] Elaine's mother did not approve of her choice of a husband, and once Elaine's father died, their relationship became even more strained. "We were pretending to be mother and daughter. We never made it beyond formalities."[2] Yet Elaine didn't cease to need her mother; she says that for years she looked for surrogate mothers. Only after her mother died did this bright, articulate woman finally make peace with her mother and herself.

Whether living or dead, our mothers are central figures in our lives. Their words, their rules, their presence—all are inscribed in our being.

As Victoria Secunda, author of *When You and Your Mother Can't Be Friends*, writes, "There is something about the painful mother-daughter relationship that can linger, for many adult daughters, with punishing tenacity. These daughters may be bright, sensitive, competent women who are valiantly trying to overcome their troubled beginnings—yet they are haunted by them, as though they had flunked childhood."[3]

How do some of us arrive at adulthood feeling that we've "flunked childhood"? If we're fearful of closeness, often swamped by feelings of inferiority, and prone either to depression or too much independence, we need to examine our emotional bond with our mothers.

I spoke with a thirty-year-old woman recently who confessed she "wasn't good at relationships" and this was hurting her career. "How's your relationship with your mother?" I asked and watched the young woman actually recoil in her seat.

"My mother's a long story," she said. "We've never been close."

As we talked, it became obvious she didn't understand the link between the mother bond and her relational difficulties with both men and women. She had never taken a close look at this relationship because it was just too painful. Besides, she felt she would be betraying her mother.

This young woman is not atypical in failing to take an honest and thoughtful look at her relationship with her mother. Nor is she alone in feeling that examining the mother/daughter knot is an act of treason. Yet if we have interpersonal pain and low self-esteem, we need to work through this primary relationship to become healthier psychologically.

Many of the women I've met in my fifty-three years have some pain to work through in their relationships with their mothers. When psychologist Mary Ainsworth and her colleagues studied infant/mother attachment relationships, about a third of those studied were insecure. One psychiatrist has said he believes only about fifty percent of parents are able to create secure attachments with their children. That means that possibly a third to a half of us were not emotionally close to our mother in childhood, and consequently we may now struggle with intimacy in our relationships, low self-esteem, and lack of confidence in coping with the exigencies of life.

Mothers who don't know how to connect

But some of us have more internal pain than others. Obviously, the emotionally or physically abusive mother creates more havoc in her daughter's life than the good, dutiful mother who simply doesn't understand how to connect emotionally. Sometimes, however, it's harder for a daughter to understand the latter. After all, her mother did many fine things for her. It feels wrong somehow to examine the relationship.

But these decent, kind women who were unable to connect with us at a deep, emotional level gave us a particular legacy that needs to be understood, or we may miss connecting with our daughters. Listen to Sandra, age fifty, a second grade teacher, describe such a mother: "Mom was friendly, loving, peaceful, but she had erected certain walls. Since I was not emotionally close to my mother, I've never talked to her about my deepest feelings and fears. Even today my mother is not comfortable with intimate conversation." Sandra adds, "I find I too have trouble letting friends and family get close."

Another woman, a forty-nine-year-old homemaker, says her practical, efficient mother met her physical needs beautifully. "But she did not provide emotional closeness, and I resented her aloofness. I have had to realize that she is emotionally handicapped, while concentrating on the good things she gave me."

Victoria Secunda describes three mothering styles that fit in this category: the doormat, the critic, the smotherer.

The doormat

According to Secunda, the doormat was the ideal mother of the 1930s. These women are "yielding. Placating. Fragile. Soft."[4] Yet they have little sense of self. "To borrow from New York Times columnist William Safire, trying to pin them down is like nailing Jell-O to a tree."[5] The doormat is deeply dependent on her husband and her children and tries to do all they ask. She has a deep sense of unworthiness, often denying her own needs. "It was this sense of unworthiness on my mother's part that I found so frightening," says educator Elaine McEwan. "I felt that her neediness would somehow suck me in and diminish my own sense of well-being and worth. I was afraid that she would ruin my marriage if my husband suspected he might have to 'parent' my mother."[6]

Doormats are not physically or emotionally abusive, but they may turn their daughters into their caregivers. Also, they provide inadequate role models to guide their daughters through the shoals of development.

The critic

These mothers constantly criticize their daughters. Their daughters never measure up, and so critics frequently punish them with silent disapproval. The critic is often at war with her own siblings, and she sabotages her daughter's friendships. She wants to keep her daughter ever dependent on her, ever seeking the love and approval she withholds. The critic uses power to keep her daughter close and guilt to maintain authority in her life. In all likelihood, the critic was herself a rejected child, and she does to her daughter what was done to her. "The zeal with which she demeans her children is a desperate attempt to salvage, by comparison, some small shard of self-esteem."[7]

Said one critic's daughter whom I interviewed, "I can never just relax or rest in my mother's presence. Besides, nothing I ever do—even as a fifty-three-year-old—is good enough. I was working in her yard the last time I visited her, and she came up behind me and redid all the gardening I had done. Will she ever be satisfied with me?" This woman adds softly, "I have been searching for the affirming mother all of my life, and I wonder what terrible thing is wrong with me."

Critics undermine their daughters' self-esteem and joy in being women. Because the critic's "victory" requires her children's diminished self-esteem, Secunda says the daughters will "defect"—be dutiful but closed, or dependent and weak.[8]

The smotherer

These women look like archetypal good mothers, but they seek to control their daughters with too much advice and too much intrusion into their lives. These mothers, who are running on empty themselves, live through their children. Unfortunately, daughters of smotherers never feel free to pursue their own lives or have their own feelings. The mothers see to that. "The smotherer," says Secunda, "wants to boost the odds that her daughters will be carefree and popular, the happiest little girls in the world."[9]

Sticking to their daughters like Velcro, these mothers deal with their own insecure maternal attachments by making their children their lives' "achievement." They do not allow their daughters to lead separate lives with their own uniqueness. Rather their daughters are their work of art.

Often the daughter of a smotherer finds she is unable to trust in friendships. Says Lucinda, "I do not confide the intimate details of my life, and I am fearful, even with females, of misunderstanding and rejection." And her husband? She admits that even he doesn't know her deepest self.

So the dutiful but emotionally inaccessible mother gives her daughter a particular kind of legacy. Since the daughter was never invited into her mother's heart, she lacks both the feelings of intimacy and the skills to generate emotional closeness. Having never learned to trust her mother with her deepest self, as an adult she holds back from other women, her spouse, and usually her own daughters.

Mothers who produce great pain

But there are other kinds of mothering experiences that also produce great pain for daughters. When our mothers were depressed, overtly rejecting, abused or physically absent, our pain is greater and our sense of loss even more profound.

The depressed mother

In a January 1994 issue of *Mademoiselle* Elizabeth Wurtzel asks, "Will I ever be happy?" Elizabeth, who takes Prozac to help with mood swings and crying spells, recounts a devastating childhood with an absent father and a severely depressed mother. After her parents' divorce, her mother was barely able to cope and held a series of marginal jobs. Elizabeth's lack of mothering has left her an "emotional nomad" who is cosmically and always homesick. Yet Elizabeth is smart enough to realize the homesickness is symptomatic of a deeper void—mother yearning—and this cannot be easily alleviated. She says, "I'm always missing someone or someplace or something. I'm always trying to get back to some imaginary somewhere. My life has been one long longing."

The rejecting mother

Some women had mothers who created enormous inner pain because they were cold and rejecting. Often they were themselves rejected or abused as children. Josie, a single woman with a graduate degree in economics, is a rejected daughter. While she describes herself as "fulfilled and happier than most," her statement rings hollow because she has suffered from chronic depression all of her life. She has no close attachments, although she has several pets. Her mother, whom she describes as "a tyrant," has seen her daughter three times in twenty years.

Susan, a divorced mother who has struggled to give her two daughters more mothering than she received, remembers her mother, also a single parent, tearing into her whenever she was harassed by life. She screamed more than once, "You're a burden, a noose, around my neck."

Secunda calls these rejecting mothers the "avengers." The avenger resembles Martha in Edward Albee's *Who's Afraid of Virginia Woolf?* She's bent on creating constant discord in her home and engages in physical and verbal battles with her husband and children. Because of her old anger resulting from physical and psychological abuse in childhood, the avenger tries to destroy her child's sense of self-worth. "Unless the daughter can summon some miraculous inner strength, or find elsewhere the supportive affection that will help her to feel good about herself—which some daughters manage to do—she will not have the will to extricate herself from her mother's tyranny."[10]

These mothers have to be center stage. Their daughters are Cinderellas who wait on their mothers, ever fearful of their mothers' rage. The avenger "rejects, isolates, terrorizes, ignores and corrupts her child."[11]

The abused mother

Sometimes women are unable to adequately mother their children because they were sexually abused in childhood. And if they failed to confront and work through their crippling guilt, pain, shame, and diminished self-esteem, they usually are not able to be close to anyone in the family. Unresolved sexual abuse in childhood may cause a mother to feel cut off from her own daughter or to worry overmuch about her daughter, lest she also be abused. Several women have told me that unresolved sexual abuse in childhood literally cut them off from everyone they held dear.

One woman used castle imagery to describe her sad experience. "Where's your husband?" I asked, entering into the imagery.

"He has just crossed the moat."

"What about your daughters?" I questioned, knowing she loved her teenagers a lot.

"Oh, they've gotten into the inner courtyard."

"And God?"

"He waits patiently on the stairs, beyond the locked door."

As I mirrored this woman's language and metaphors, I suggested to my friend that one day, with God's help, she would throw open the shutters and unlock the door of her lonely tower room. Her family could then come inside to celebrate her healing and her new life. She would welcome God into her little room.

Over time this has happened to a great extent. As this friend shared her shameful secrets with a trusted few, she was gradually freed from those crippling feelings of guilt and shame and was able to reach out to her family.

Moreover, at last she was able to experience God's love and healing. That castle room has long since been abandoned for a life with more intimate connections to her husband, daughters, and friends.

The lost mother

But childhood trauma is not the only experience that prevents a mother from establishing secure ties to her children. Sometimes mothers are simply gone. And their physical absence, for whatever reason, means their children took graduate courses in loneliness and depression.

Ten o'clock in the morning. My new client is Sarah, an attractive woman in her mid thirties whose husband has just died of a massive heart attack. This loss reopens an early wound. "My mother died when I was three," she says, wiping her cheeks carefully to avoid smudging her mascara. "Oh, how I've missed her over the years. I need her now." She is quiet for a moment, then adds in a little girl voice, her face contorted and childlike, "You never outgrow your need for a mother."

Sarah is right. We never outgrow our *need* for our mothers. And if we lose our mothers, either temporarily or forever, when we are young, at some level we never quite get over this. To lose our mothers to death is to lose a part of ourselves. It is not only to lose the primary nurturer of our earliest years, it is to lose the one who knows more about us than anyone else. Mother is the family historian; she is also the guide we need to teach us about adolescence, parenting, marriage. Some of us—women and men—feel keenly the effects of this loss all of our lives, especially if we did not have a warm, accepting surrogate mother step in and give us the love we needed.

The movie *Shadowlands,* based on the life of Oxford don C. S. Lewis, is a case in point. Lewis's mother died when he was a vulnerable nine-year-old, and Lewis was left in the care of a mercurial, unstable father. Lewis spent most of his adult life as a bachelor, teaching first at Oxford and later at Cambridge, though he is best known for his prolific writing, particularly his Narnia stories and Christian apologetics. Lewis befriended a difficult American divorcée named Joy Gresham. And, in his sixties, Lewis married Joy as she was dying of cancer. Finally, Lewis experienced the love that had eluded him since his mother's untimely death. Joy taught him that true love and intimacy inevitably involve a measure of pain. "The happiness now is part of the pain to follow," said Joy shortly after their marriage. And after her death, Lewis understood and accepted the reality of her words. At the movie's end, Lewis cried, not only for Joy and himself, but also, I suspect, for his mother.

From my own life I know that maternal loss in childhood is devastating and can leave the daughter with a deep sense of longing. Years ago a friend gave me a tape of the song "My Mother" by Amanda McBroom, who also wrote "The Rose," which Bette Midler made famous. In this haunting autobiographical song, McBroom captures the yearning, the emptiness, the diminished self-esteem of the daughter who has lost a beloved mother to death in childhood. "Mama, don't leave me. Mama, please stay. Mama, I need you to show me the way. I'm lost and I'm lonely and I can't find my way any more." "Mama" wails McBroom in the haunting final moment of the song. I cannot listen to this song without feeling a knot in the pit of my stomach. Admittedly, the song touches my own deepest self, for not only did my mother leave me for three years in the care of my grandmother, but my mother lost her mother to death when she was four. Whenever I heard my mother speak about Martha Callie Bradford, it was in a voice laced with longing.

Absence makes the whole heart hurt

"The young child's hunger for his mother's love and presence is as great as his hunger for food,"[12] wrote psychiatrist John Bowlby. A baby's need for her mother is so great that even temporary absence "inevitably generates 'a powerful sense of loss and anger.'"[13] While Bowlby was not referring to the brief, daily absences that have been the experience of many in the twenty-something generation, child development experts worry about the long-term effects of early and continuing substitute care in a child's life, particularly if begun in the first year. A number of researchers have found that if babies are in substitute care for more than twenty hours per week during that first year of life, they are at risk for insecure attachment to mothers and/or fathers.

While separation is hard on daughters, it's also hard on mothers. An article in *Family Circle* in March, 1994 captures poignantly the tears in the mother/daughter relationship that may ensue when the mother is too often absent from her children's lives. Joyce Wood, a lawyer who left her firstborn, Louise, when she was six weeks old and her second daughter, Rebecca, at twelve weeks, describes this wrenching experience from a mother's perspective in an essay ironically called "Quality Time":

> Every year in February or March, when the days are short and life is bleak, I'm overtaken by regrets. I spend weeks having second thoughts. I wish I'd stayed home when my kids were small.... At this time of year, I want to take it all back and start over. I become convinced that I made the wrong choice.... In the first few days back at the office, I could feel my milk coming in at feeding time, and it broke my heart.
>
> My poor babies were like Romulus and Remus without even a wolf for a mother (because I was busy keeping the wolf from the door). No wonder they're savages. Sometimes when Louise (at 15) blows orange juice from her nostrils to amuse her friends, I find myself thinking, "Why doesn't someone take this child aside?" Then I realize I'm the one who is supposed to do it.
>
> Poor Louise. My husband used to call her Attila the Baby. When she was in a high chair and should have been learning what orange juice is for, I was away on a business trip.... I had planned to go right back to work, so that was that. I operated like a man in those days. Plans were vital and not to be veered from. Emotion was suspect, a thing to be squashed....
>
> My work track paid off...and all I feel is that my children are nearly grown and gone and I missed out.... My kids were raised by levitation, not by me.

This is not to say that all mothers who work full-time feel as Wood did or that they have emotionally insecure daughters. Far from it. Many daughters of employed moms do just fine, and many moms have no regrets. But we do ourselves and others a great disservice if we deny the possibility of negative effects on our emotions and our hearts that can accrue from repeated, daily absences, particularly when we were very young.

What's at issue here is something quite subtle. For mothers to be tuned in emotionally to their children requires that they be not just physically present but also emotionally present. Depression, fatigue, high adrenaline, pressures to meet deadlines—all interfere with a mother's ability to tune in to her child, listen, and effectively meet the child's needs.

One of my friends who is currently home with three gorgeous little boys told me of a month recently when she was preparing a highly documented speech and was subtly detached from her children. "Even when I was with them, I wasn't there. My mind was elsewhere. After a while I didn't feel as close to them as before. I started to disconnect." She added, "Emotional intimacy is a subtle thing."

Prolonged maternal absence

While brief, daily absences can create emotional distance and insecurity, prolonged maternal absence leaves an even greater imprint. When mothers are separated from their young children over a long period of time, not only do their young children lose touch with them, but a woman's feelings of maternal love are apt to cool.

In our own era as women have gone into combat for the first time in our nation, we have witnessed separation of mothers and their infants due to war. Who can forget the anguish on the mothers' faces as they prepared to leave their children, even babies, for Desert Storm? Who can forget the poignant story of Holly Vallance who cradled her seven-week-old daughter in her arms as she prepared to leave Fort Benning, Georgia, for the Middle East? Clad in helmet and fatigues, Holly said, "I never dreamed anything like this would happen in my lifetime, let alone right after I had had my first child. I have built an ice wall around my heart to try to cool the pain, and sometimes I worry that Tony and Cheyenne won't be able to melt it away."

A wall of ice.

Some ice walls never melt. And when a daughter misses out on mother love and nurturance so desperately needed, she too learns to build a wall around her heart to protect her vulnerable self. She may learn to push others away. In time, she may find herself isolated and lonely, unable to connect at a deep emotional level.

As we push for drastic changes in our culture, we need to evaluate career and the whole issue of women's rights in light of another important facet of women's lives: motherhood. No career should come before the needs of children's hearts and emotions. Otherwise, the psychological price we both pay is just too high.

The unmothered legacy

British psychoanalyst Anthony Storr suggests we need to experience enough "irrational devotion" from our parents to feel reasonably whole. If we didn't get this or if our parents set impossibly high standards which we could not meet, we may have failed to develop an inner sense of worth. As a consequence, we may be prone to depression, too dependent on the good opinion of others, and too fearful of their criticism. Overanxious to please, we will not be as assertive as we need to be to work on our intimate relationships.[14]

If we are deprived of sufficient mothering for any reason, we arrive on the doorstep of adulthood with open, empty hands. In her book *Of Women Born* Adrienne Rich says, "The woman who has felt 'unmothered' may seek mothers all her life—may even seek them in men. Some of us marry, looking for a mother."[15] Or we may deny this absence of mothering by becoming caretakers ourselves; we may become teachers, doctors, political activists, or psychotherapists. In that way we give to others what was not given to us—but this solution has its down side. When a woman does this, says Rich, "this will always mean that she needs the neediness of others in order to go on feeling her own strength. She may feel uneasy with equals—particularly women."[16]

So what are we to do?

So what do we do if the mother knot is painful?

At the mental health clinic where I work, we say, "What we don't work out, we act out." This is particularly true in the area of mothering. It's important that we understand the legacy our mothers gave us and work through any pain. Only then can we find healing. Only then will we be free.

For as Victoria Secunda writes, if we fail to resolve a painful mother/daughter relationship, we will befriend people who share our mother's destructive tendencies or we may reject those who remind us of our mothers. Worse, we may marry men who are our mother's twin. And our children? We may turn them into the caregivers we never had, burdening them with our secrets, trying to use their love to fill the hole in our soul. Finally, we will be unable to set healthy boundaries with those women who continue to wound us.[17]

Sometimes a daughter wakes up and says, "Enough of this longing. I want to work through my mother yearning so I can give my children more love and security than was given to me. I don't want to continue to destroy my marriage or hate myself." With that awareness—that declaration of psychological independence—a woman beings to confront the pain in earnest. She begins to make peace with her mother. She begins to make peace with herself.

5

• • •

Making Peace with Our Mothers

The unending paradox is that we do learn through pain.

Madeleine L'Engle

L isa is emotionally cut off from her rejecting mother. When Lisa was growing up, her mother criticized her frequently: Lisa ate too much, was slow in school, and didn't have good manners. Sometimes to "encourage" her daughter to lose weight, Lisa's mother bought her dresses that were too small and refused to return them. So Lisa, who already thought she was ugly and fat, merely ate more.

By the time Lisa was an adult, she was a hundred pounds overweight. Inside her body hid a fragile woman who laughed too much (if she kept people happy, they wouldn't notice her weight), worked too hard (if she accomplished a lot, she would deserve her place on earth), and strove to please (would someone, anyone, give her the love and approval she so desperately needed?).

Over the years Lisa simply stopped writing to her mother and eventually stopped seeing her. She and her husband began a peripatetic existence, moving from state to state, further and further from her parental home. Both were busy in corporate careers. And when her mother begged to see her, Lisa made excuses to keep her at bay.

At the same time, Lisa turned her three daughters into her emotional caregivers. They had to help their hungry mother deal with her psychological problems; they had to nurture her while denying their own emotional needs. Lisa's daughters complied because this was the only way they could get any love and attention from their mother. But it was a high price to pay. One became outwardly resentful even as she continually built up her mother in person and over the phone. She has decided never to have any children herself. After all, who really mothered her?

Now fifty-five, Lisa is considering examining her relationship with her mother. She senses that coming to terms with her mother will mean hard psychological work: she would have to go beyond her fear, rage, and blame to confront her deep-seated pain. But something healthy inside longs to be free and finally come to terms with her mother.

Coming to terms with our mother

What's involved in coming to terms with our mother? *I believe we must begin to see the relationship as it really is, not as we wish it to be.* To do this, we must be willing to take a long, hard, honest look at our relationship with our mother. If we have been deeply wounded, we may have learned to deny our pain or to tell ourselves lies about our childlike dependencies on our mother. So it won't be easy to see ourselves as we are. Or we may have dealt with our mother by seeing ourselves as victims, ever blaming our mother for the responsible choices we have refused to make. But it does no real good to remain a victim. We cease to grow, we whine, we drive others away.

At this point, you may shrug hopelessly and say, "My mother will never change, so why bother?" The truth is we can change, and if we do, our relationship with our mother must, of necessity, change. We will never be the women we were meant to be as long as we are locked in struggles with our mothers—even in our heads—or we are submerging our personalities to win love too long withheld. And if our mother is dead? It is never too late to make peace with ourselves.

One of my friends, a sunny eighty-six-year-old, and I had a wonderful conversation about three weeks before she died. As I sat on her bed, we talked openly about death, and my friend was serene except for some unfinished business. "I've just realized this week how much I resented my mother who was abrupt and harsh. I need to forgive her," she said. "It's been painful to realize I've carried this bitterness so long." We talked, and she was able to let go of her resentment. As long as we are alive, it is never too late to free ourselves of anger and bitterness.

A woman clutches a yellowed letter covered with faded ink, a letter written by her mother when she was twenty-two to her mother-in-law. She tells me haltingly that she has just found proof of what she has felt all her life. I read:

Dear Mrs. Benson:

Jim is sleeping on the couch so he won't have to look after the baby at night. She sleeps with me and cries all night. I'll be glad when I can put her on a bottle and turn her over to Jim. I had her for him anyway and it's not my fault she wasn't a boy. It's been raining up here for a week. Am glad to see the sun shining today. Jim says I don't care nothing about the baby. He promised me some new clothes, but now he has backed out. I'm going shopping anyway.

That's all for now.

See you in three months,

Love, Ruby

After we read the letter together, my friend wept and said, "I *knew* it. I just knew it. I've always felt mother didn't love me and here's the proof." She is just beginning an inner journey to confront the feelings of "unlove" and rejection she has carried all her life. If she is brave and doesn't simply pull away from her mother, she has a chance to achieve greater wholeness.

But she must recognize the fact that her young, uneducated, emotionally deprived mother had little nurture to give. She also needs to acknowledge, in the company of a caring person, what she never received—the love and acceptance which is every child's birthright. And she needs to grieve.

One woman whose mother was sometimes crazy remembers her therapist yelling at her, "Let her go. She'll never give you the love you want. You'd get more love from a dog." Although the woman bridled at his comparison of her mother and a dog, the psychologist hit a nerve. She went home and sobbed for two days. The enormity of her mother's emotional abuse hung heavy in the air around her. She felt the weight of all she had missed of mother love. As she described it, "After two days of crying—deep, guttural sobs—I finally wound down. For a while I felt peaceful but empty. I knew I had been cleansed. Days later I realized I was sleeping at night. No more haunting dreams. No more demons to exorcise. No more pain."

Coming to terms with both our mothers

Although it is never easy to come to terms with our mother, maybe it will help to understand that we are, in truth, dealing with *two* mothers. When I asked Dr. David Allen about this subject, he said, "A woman needs to understand that there are two mothers—the actual, external mother and the internalized one." To make peace with our mothers, Allen believes we must first make peace with ourselves. "Some women actually join with their abusing mothers to beat themselves up and hate themselves." When that happens, Allen asks the woman, "Must you continue to abuse yourself as your mother once did?" A woman must first deal with the issues of her own heart before she deals with her mother.

So what's involved in dealing with the issues of our own hearts? We need to realize that our mother passed on the mothering she received. When a female client talks to me about her relationship with her mother, I often ask her about her mother's relationship with her grandmother. Her eyes usually light up when she "sees" how inadequate mothering may have been passed down through three generations.

Finding forgiveness

Once we understand that our mothers may have been denied maternal love and approval, it becomes easier to forgive them for what they didn't give us and for the hurt they inflicted. Forgiveness is never easy. And it isn't cheap. It cost Christ his life to forgive those who hurt and eventually killed him. But forgiveness is essential for our emotional health. As the nineteenth century Scottish minister George MacDonald said, "It may be infinitely less evil to murder a man than to refuse to forgive him. The former may be the act of a moment of passion: the latter is the heart's choice."[1]

Until we can forgive, we are slaves to our bitterness and anger. How do we forgive? Fortunately, we don't have to wait to feel like forgiving someone who has hurt us. In fact, when faced with the possibility of forgiving, our feelings may threaten mutiny. But once we elect to forgive, no matter how treacherous the wrong, we discover that feelings follow action. To withhold forgiveness is to wither spiritually.

Psychotherapist Novie Hinson feels that forgiveness is a gift we give ourselves. She says her definition of forgiveness means "I am no longer looking to the one who hurt me to make it up to me. If I forgive someone, I no longer look to that person to change or apologize—that leaves me stuck in my anger and pain. Forgiveness can be a selfish thing in a good sort of way. It's saying, 'I release you; I'm not looking for you to make me okay.'" Hinson continues, "When I forgive, I make the decision to look to God to make things right. The person who hurt me is no longer God in my life."

While Hinson is clear that forgiveness is a unilateral decision of the will, she is firm about what forgiveness is not. "Forgiveness is not continuing on in an unhealthy relationship. We can't say, 'I'll forgive you so we can go back to being unhealthy again.'"

In Hinson's schema, forgiveness is not condoning the wrong nor is it forgetting. She acknowledges that sometimes we can't forget. "That's a psychiatric disorder called amnesia," she laughs. "But once we forgive, we don't lie awake rehearsing the wrongs anymore. If we're rehearsing, we're stuck. We're trying to get the other person to see it our way—to make us okay. Since forgiveness is not an emotion, we may still feel angry about the event and its repercussions for some time."

What about reconciliation? Hinson acknowledges that the church teaches restoration of the relationship to the pre-event status. "But that means going back to an unhealthy relationship," she says. She adds, "Some people simply refuse to be reconciled. As for the mother/daughter relationship, that's a tangled web. And if a mother continues to rule her daughter or if she's abusive, sometimes there can't be true reconciliation. There can't be full reconciliation and restoration until the party who caused the injury takes full ownership of the wrong."

Once we forgive and set healthy boundaries in our relationship with our mother, we often discover that our mother—who may fight us tooth and nail at first—is relieved. Establishing healthy boundaries allows our mother to relate to us as adults, and together we reclaim something of the mother/daughter relationship that has been denied us.

Rachel's tale

Rachel remembers that her mother spent her nights drunk on the floor from the time Rachel was twelve until she married in her twenties. Because she challenged her mother, Rachel became the target of her mother's wrath. "Most of my childhood memories of my mother are negative—harsh spankings, being called 'a bull in a china closet.' In second grade I wrote on my headboard, 'I hate my mother.' Dad favored me and she resented it. My high school years were very painful. She used to lock me out late at night if she was drunk, hide my favorite clothes, and tell my friends I wasn't home when they called. It was hurtful to have my mother view me as an enemy and to feel we were engaged in guerrilla warfare. I was always on guard and couldn't trust her."

Now at forty-five, Rachel continues to rework her relationship with her mother. "Several years ago I realized that she owed me an enormous debt she could never repay—*my lost childhood.* As I saw this, I knew I had a choice—I could hold her hostage to this debt or relinquish its collection. If I kept her hostage, I would carry feelings of anger and bitterness toward her forever. About this time I read Matthew 18 and was struck by Jesus' parable of the lord who forgave his servant millions while that same servant refused to forgive another man the little he owed. As I read, I felt God had forgiven my huge debt, so I had to forgive my mother's smaller one. I also saw that if I forgave her, I could finally begin to heal. I chose to forgive. Afterwards, for the first time in memory, I began to feel some emotional warmth toward my mother.

"Now we talk regularly on the phone, and I am sincerely interested in her. But I never share intimate or deep feelings with her. It's not safe. However, I feel I've made peace with her at last."

Rachel has discovered what all of us must if we will ever be free. We must forgive again and again the big wrongs and the little injuries. The alternative—holding on to hatred and bitterness—will eventually do us in and hurt our relationships with our own daughters as well.

I saw a client once who came because she was unable to forge a close bond with her three-year-old daughter. She felt an unreasoning rage toward her little girl and often yelled at her and pushed her away, to which the child responded with tantrums. When I asked this woman about her relationship with her own mother, she looked at me defiantly and said, "I have a terrible relationship with my mother, and I have no intention of forgiving her." Not surprisingly, she didn't stay in therapy long. If improving her relationship with her daughter meant she would need to work on her relationship with her mother, she preferred to forego therapy.

Peace at last

Fortunately, many of us do the hard work of getting free from the bondage to the past. We make peace with the internalized mother, in part through forgiveness, which works its alchemy in our souls. And then a wonderful thing happens. We see clearly, sometimes for the first time, the gifts our mother gave us. Before, we were too absorbed in our inner turmoil to fully appreciate what we've accrued from being our mother's daughters.

It was only after she had made peace with her mother (even though her mother was dead), that Elaine McEwan realized her mother had given her and her sister "wonderful gifts of affirmation, acceptance, caring and respect. She had done that for us, and we were able to do it for our children. In my haste to blame and separate from my mother, I had failed to affirm and recognize that my ability to write books about parenting, my ability to teach children with patience, and my ability to respect each child as an individual came from her.... I only regretted that it was too late to tell my mother in person."[2]

Her words are instructive. Most of us would prefer to make peace with our mothers while they are still alive so we can enjoy the relationship. This does not mean, however, that we can't make peace with a mother who is no longer living. One woman, after she had dealt with her anger and grief and had developed some compassion for herself, went to her mother's grave, raged, and wept. She left the graveside that day lighter and happier than she had felt in years.

And, as I discovered when I worked through my own mother yearning, once we go beyond our resentment and embrace the good our mother gave us, we feel better about ourselves and our sex.

We also can begin to appreciate the fact, as it says in Psalm 139, that God has known us from the womb—that He, in fact, chose the womb that housed us. He gives us the mothers we have. This is not to say God condones abuse, rejection, manipulation. But if we believe He *knows* us and has a plan for our human lives, our mothers are part and parcel of that plan.

I came to see that life with my mother, painful as it was at times, shaped much of who I am today. Our relationship—with its positive and negative characteristics—has fueled my desire to understand mothering, my interest in helping young, unnurtured mothers care for their babies, and my deep desire to give my girls more than my mother, because of her wounds, was able to give me. My early life continues to drive my concern for children who are growing up without close emotional bonds with their mothers.

With that realization came a sense of peace. And in the days and months that followed, I felt more whole. An old, familiar ache had gone. Something inside had gone quiet.

Coming to terms with my mother positively affected my relationship with my husband, Don, and my daughters. Less anxious, dependent, and needy, I became more autonomous. My family had greater freedom to *be*. That happened ten years ago, and I can truthfully say I no longer feel any pain from my childhood.

What a world of difference forgiveness makes. We can, at last, let the past go. As C. S. Lewis says, "Notice in Dante that the lost souls are entirely concerned about their past. Not so the saved."

So let us move into the present—forgiving and forgiven. As Dr. Allen says, "We must take charge of our hearts." Only then do we know peace—at last.

◆　◆　◆

Karen's Story

With her mane of glossy chestnut hair and impossibly thin figure, Karen, at forty-two, looks like a Ralph Lauren model. She is beautiful, warm, and chic. Ever adventurous, she has camped alone in Montana and rafted down the rivers of New Mexico. Her work as a stockbroker brings her in contact with a variety of interesting people. If you were to meet her, you would never guess that this woman has been anything but sunny about her eclectic life. But at forty, Karen faced a personal crisis. Uncertain about her future and unhappy with her relationship with her mother, Karen left one Christmas on a personal quest. Here is her story:

The morning I left my mother, we argued again about my leaving. She told me that I was ruining Christmas for her. She could not understand my feelings—the loneliness and fear I had had ever since moving from Washington, D.C. to live under her roof.

Various circumstances had led me to return to my hometown. I sensed a purpose in it but was unsure what it was. Having recently turned forty, with no job and no sense of career direction, no close friends nearby, and no romantic prospects, I felt especially hopeless. Nothing was going as I had expected. It was as if I had backed into a cul-de-sac but had lost the entrance. In my mental state, Christmas parties and cheery chatter were more than I could endure. I had to get away. The daughter of an acquaintance had agreed to let me stay on her ranch in the New Mexico mountains, alone, for three weeks. It was a gift from heaven.

As I drove to Santa Fe, I knew I was not headed for a time of festivities, fun on the ski slopes, or escape into a novel by a fireplace, but for a time of introspection. Though I had been away from my family for several years, the old problems between my mother and me had not disappeared. In fact, they seemed more present than ever. The hope that family could provide understanding and support was disappointed daily. My Christian faith had resiliently weathered some tough times but was now at its lowest ebb. I kept repeating, "God is here and He loves me," but this had become a refrain without a melody. It was a relief to leave Mom, to be able to cry as I drove west, without suffering through Mom's fussing and tips on how to be your own best friend. Mom always picked up on any hint of sadness and viewed it as a cue for action. She did all she could to "fix" me. And when her efforts didn't work, she became angry. Mom hated to fail.

The second morning of the trip I drove up the winding mountain road to the ranch. The landscape was unimpressive: brown snow along the muddy road, sparse shrubs, and scrubby evergreens. Nothing grand or awe-inspiring. Yet the barren winter scene was oddly comforting. It seemed to correspond with my feelings. At the gateway to the ranch I stopped my car to look around. Low mountains covered with trees and snow surrounded a valley in which the ranch was nestled. A stream flowed through the middle of the property, covering the road with icy patches. The ranch itself was small—five adobe buildings. There was a main house, a barn, a manager's quarters, a chapel, and the small adobe house where I would stay. Everyone had already left for Christmas except the manager who met me to give a brief orientation. As she left she said, "Call me if you need anything. Otherwise, you're on your own."

During the following days, I engaged in simple tasks: cooking, tending the fire, hiking in the mountains, reading my Bible, and praying. These activities gave me a sense of order. They replaced my frenetic energy with a rhythmic calm. The perfect quiet was broken only by occasional motors humming in the distance, bird sounds, and coyotes howling at night. Snow fell each day. I began listening to my heart, and more tentatively still, listening to God. When I awoke each morning, I pulled on my clothes and walked to the chapel to pray. The tiny room had bare walls. A rough Indian rug and pillows lay on a tile floor. A worn, wooden table served as the altar. Between two candles stood a primitive wooden crucifix. Its simplicity soothed my heart. Each night I looked out of the bedroom window in my adobe house to see a spotlight illumining the chapel doorway and bell tower. This was the only light in the dark valley and the last thing I saw at night. I adopted this nighttime image as a metaphor for my life: "The light shines in the darkness, and the darkness has not overcome it."[3] This light was true.

For the first time in months I felt God's presence and a sense of gratitude. I realized that He had drawn me aside to face up to issues which had affected every relationship I had ever had. Here I was, an adult, independent for the past seventeen years, yet still subject to my relationship with my mother and the power it exerted over me.

During those days at the ranch, I looked clearly at the relationship with my mother for the first time. I abandoned the "If only you had…" or "Why can't you be…" and even the "Why can't we…" for a different viewpoint—reality. I realized that as a single woman, I still had an extraordinarily strong craving to be a child, to let her fix my problems. It was scary to be alone in the world. Scary to have no husband to rely on. My mother had become an oasis of comfort and protection. As tightly as I clung to her, I bitterly resented her. I longed to please her but always fell short. The Bs I had earned in school and life did not meet her perfectionistic standards. Our relationship exacted a high price. For me, it meant a diminished trust in God and a lack of confidence in my own abilities. It also created internal anger that I allowed her approval to influence me, yet my obedience was necessary for her contentment.

My mother takes great pride in her accomplishments, which include her children. Our success and happiness are her major concerns. If we aren't experiencing both simultaneously, she takes action. Mother has often gone where angels fear to tread. She loves with passion and practicality, but without intimacy. She blesses and she wounds. She is good and she is sinful. She is wise and she is foolish. As I reached these revelations, I also realized that I could never hope to change her. *I could only change myself if I wanted our relationship to be different.* Part of this involved changing my perspective of her from an "idol" to a fellow human being.

Those three weeks on the ranch began a personal transformation. In confronting my relationship with my mother, I confronted myself. In the months since, I have realized that my mother will never be able to repay the debt of nurture and acceptance she owes me, but I have carved out a new relationship with her.

This has not been easy. Every inch has been contested. I know at times I hurt my mother deeply as she resists new patterns of relating. But through it all we are learning to respect each other. Sometimes she actually seems relieved to be confronted. At times I still long to crawl into her lap and be held like I never was as a child. Though that time has passed, I can accept and forgive my mother. While we still argue and fail miserably at our attempts to love each other, we can also spontaneously hug each other. This is a new and wonderful thing!

Although the loneliness of being single can be intense, an inner security is gradually replacing my fear. I know this change is permanent. I am not sure these changes would have ever occurred had I not moved back to live in my hometown. While the old adage says that mothers "cut the apron strings," I believe that sometimes daughters must take up that task.

Karen says she now feels better about herself than she ever has—that she had to come home to be able, finally, to leave home.

6

. . .

Daughters:
Our Mirror Images

Thou art thy mother's glass, she in thee

calls back the lovely April of her prime.

Shakespeare, sonnet III

The day had finally come. When my daughter Kristen picked me up in her little red sedan, we headed for Old Town, Alexandria. Two women, one quest. We were in search of the perfect wedding gown for Kristen and Greg's wedding, six months hence. As we drove, Kristen, peaceful but excited, said that she had prayed earlier for our "bonding experience."

Looking up from *Bride's* magazine I nodded, knowing that Kristen and I sometimes vehemently disagree. Today, I determined, my role was simple: to be supportive of her choice.

We headed for a large bridal shop that friends had recommended. The shop consists of different rooms with differently priced gowns. Here, the bride-to-be is shown only what she has said she can afford.

After we had declared our price range, Kim, a soothing Iranian, ushered us into an empty room, and the search began. Kris tried on dress after dress. Early on, she found one she liked—a lovely, beaded affair with a long train. At my request she also tried on a Grace Kellyesque gown with a flowing skirt and a gorgeous top of German lace, long sleeves, and a sweetheart neckline. While I felt the effect was stunning, Kris thought the dress too plain. So she completed the paperwork on the beaded dress, and we went to lunch.

As we sat in a cozy Italian restaurant, Kris said anxiously, "This has been too easy. My friends have had to try on hundreds of dresses to find *the* dress. Maybe I haven't seen enough gowns."

Sensing her buyer's remorse, I suggested we go to another shop, one that turned out to be dingy and cramped. Soon Kristen was ensconced in a dressing room with a woman three times her size yelling in her ear.

As the search continued, Kristen emerged from the room in gown after gown, looking like exhausted quarry. When she finally found a too expensive gown she liked, the saleswoman and proprietor surrounded her like hunters going in for the kill. Kris looked at me beseechingly, and I rose from my chair, put my arm around my daughter, and said, "Kris is tired. Maybe we need to go have a cup of tea and think about this."

"Thanks, Mom, I needed you," said my grateful daughter moments later. "Now I feel I've worked hard enough. Let's go back to the first shop."

Soon we were once again in Kim's presence as Kris tried on her choice as well as the beautiful gown I loved. By this time Kris had changed her mind. The other saleswoman had convinced her that she looked better in simpler, elegant gowns rather than promlike dresses. As Kris tried on the elegant silk shantung, we said in unison, "That's it! That's the dress." And when Kim placed the beaded tiara and veil on my daughter's head, scooping up her hair, I cried. My daughter was transformed. Gone the fatigue, the hesitancy, the worry. Instead, Kristen stood before me a radiant bride.

It was a magical moment, just as friends with married daughters had said it would be. And in the background, as if she had read my mind, I could hear Kim's quiet comment, "It's a Grace Kelly kind of gown."

Women's love for their daughters

I am passionate when it comes to my daughters. In an era when career is glorified and children's needs minimized, rearing my two daughters has been one of the most challenging and rewarding experiences of my life. None of my accomplishments compares with this joy.

My love affair with my children began before they were born. In fact,

I used to tease them by saying I had known them from the womb. "Gag, Mom!" was usually the response from these junior highers. I was amused. They didn't understand that as a teenager I didn't even particularly like children and that later I had children because in the sixties it was the expected thing for a young married woman to do.

But my daughters—with their love, demands, and occasional surliness—have changed me forever. And I am the better for it.

Even today as I sit in Lauinger Library at Georgetown University in a carrel surrounded by books on mothers and daughters, I can still remember the glow that surrounded Holly's birth. Two years later, I welcomed a second daughter into the world, a month early and in the breech position. Kristen was, even in the womb, different from her sister. While Holly was known for her easy movements and occasional bumps, Kristen had athletic thumps and rapid-fire movement, particularly in the last trimester of the pregnancy. My husband and I thought we had a future athlete on our hands.

Today my daughters are grown women. Compassionate, deeply moral, and responsible, they are two quite different and lovely beings. Holly has been my literary child—reading, writing short stories, attending summer writing programs. Even now she produces publications and designs graphics for a corporation. Kristen, a social being and fine student who reads under duress, works for a Washington, D.C. think tank. She loves the scrap and heat of national politics and often calls to tell me what just came off the Political Hot Line.

But I am not unusual in my passion for my daughters. Listen to the comments of some of the women I interviewed:

Mary Ellen, thirty-four: "I am blessed to have a nine-year-old daughter. We are very close, and I take great care to make sure she can open up and tell me anything. We share special interests: ice skating, theater...roller blading."

Karey, forty-three: "I feel we are quite close, just as I was with my mom. We enjoy being together. We laugh and have lots of fun. My daughter shares all her school and friend frustrations and 'boy things.' Our battle is basically having time to spend together."

Leona, fifty: "My daughter and I are extremely close. Recently my husband paid me the highest compliment. He said my motherhood was my crowning achievement. My daughter and I love and respect each other, while maintaining our boundaries. It's a healthy, loving, and mutually nurturing relationship."

Alice, seventy: "I am close to both my daughters. I had a difficult time when one was nineteen, but after a night of prayer I wrote her a long letter, asking forgiveness for my failures as a mother and telling her about the relationship I hoped for. She wrote a beautiful letter in return, and we have grown steadily closer."

We see ourselves in our daughters

As mothers, we invariably see ourselves in our daughters—an identification that begins in infancy. Our daughters share our sex. Their bodies, though small, look familiar. As they mature, we understand their developmental needs and changes. We too were once little girls who played for hours with our dolls and fought with our siblings. We loved our friends and longed to have them sleep over. Said one mother the day after she and her husband had driven five twelve-year-olds to the mall, "Sometimes I am amused by their squeals and laughter and endless gossip. At least, I once was a twelve-year-old girl myself. My husband seldom finds a group of twelve-year-old girls amusing! Exasperating, yes."

As our daughters grow, we have another chance to read *Wind in the Willows, Little Women* and *Jo's Boys* along with them. We can, without guilt, spend lazy summer days hanging out at the public library or the swimming pool, chatting with their friends and ours. With them we re-discover the mall through a preteen's eyes.

When our girls become teenagers, we commiserate with PMS and zits and the diminished self-esteem that tracks the hormonal cycle. Like them, we thought the telephone was a device Alexander Graham Bell invented just so we could stay connected with our girlfriends. With them we shop for prom dresses and eventually a wedding dress.

Mothering through the teenage years

But let's stop here for a minute and just be honest. Mothering teenagers can be tough, and is definitely harder for some of us than others.

My friend Susan Yates, author along with her husband John of *What Really Matters at Home,* has found adolescence her favorite season of child rearing. A mother of five, Susan feels her children's early years were the hardest because "there's so much training involved and you don't see immediate payback." But when her daughters became teenagers, they began to become friends. "You start relating gradually to teenagers as peers rather than as total parent. If you've been firm with them as young children, in their late teens they're delightful people who begin to know who they are."

Susan—with a twenty-two-year-old daughter, Allison, and fifteen-year-old twins, Susie and Libby—has also made a point of getting to know her children's friends. "I want to know what their friends are into, what they're going to do in the summer, what their favorite classes are." She says one of Allison's friends at William and Mary recently called out of the blue. "She just wanted to touch base and find out how I was, and that blesses my daughter."

Susan often asks her adolescent sons—John is nineteen and Chris is seventeen—to pray for her. She and her husband, the senior minister at the Falls Church Episcopal, in Falls Church, Virginia, started this practice when their children were young. "Even a small child can pray, 'Dear God, help Mommy today,'" says Susan.

In addition, both John and Susan believe in lots and lots of hugs. "Saying 'I love you' often sounds so basic," says Susan, "but you'd be surprised how few parents do that. Since our kids were small, we've given them lots of physical affection, and we've had open, honest communication. I made a practice of curling up in bed with both sons and daughters to hear them share their secrets. And I've told my daughters they're beautiful and helped them fix themselves up. If we don't tell them, they'll listen to someone else."

While I applaud Susan's values, I must admit I found adolescence the toughest years of parenting my daughters. Why? I'm sure the fact that they had gone with me through a divorce and remarriage made things harder for all of us. After all, adolescence is the time when the psychological chickens come home to roost, so to speak. During this period my girls began separating from me with a vengeance, and they weren't particularly interested in being seen with me in public or anywhere else for that matter. Kristen was quite sure she didn't want to be seen with her mother in the mall. She told me flippantly I could walk in front or behind her. Boy, was I angry. Where was the adoring ten-year-old who loved to spend time with her mother?

My friend Phyllis tried to comfort me by saying my daughters would become my friends just about the time they went off to college. To a large extent, this did happen. My stock, which so radically dropped in high school, began slowly to climb, and in college Kris called every other day just to chat. Holly decided that once a week was enough to talk to any parent.

For those of you who struggle with teenage daughters, let me share friends' advice which I later learned was grounded in psychological research. They told me to give my daughters greater freedom but to continue to be firm and hold the line on strategic issues. They also suggested that my husband and I needed to present a united front, particularly in the area of discipline. They encouraged me to reach out and either find or create a support group of other mothers. This latter suggestion helped me greatly as the girls were leaving home. Friends are our lifelines when our daughters are separating and we are facing the empty nest and renegotiating our marriages.

Finally, friends encouraged me to remember how I felt as an adolescent trying to forge an identity and gather strength to leave home. For women who had high functioning families, this is helpful advice. But for those of us from low functioning families, too much identification may have its dark side.

The dark side of identification

Because the mother/daughter relationship is the most intense in the family system,[1] it is possible to become enmeshed with our daughters. We may want them to have the fulfilling lives that eluded us or push them to achieve in ways we lacked the courage to pursue. I have been struck by the number of unhappy traditional mothers I have known who have pushed their daughters into uninterrupted career success. One woman who was trapped in an abusive marriage told her two daughters, "Work. Always work. Never stay home with your children full-time like I did." Her daughters have followed their mother's instruction. Both are well-educated professionals who earn high salaries. One, a lawyer, is childless. The other, a university professor, has worked throughout her five children's lives. Neither has bothered to ask: am I living the life I choose, or am I living out my mother's fears and frustrations?

As mothers, we need to allow our daughters to develop their gifts and follow their hearts. We are only their cheerleaders, not the shapers of their destiny.

It's also important that we not project our unresolved psychological dilemmas onto our daughters. Fran, a reformed flower child, went ballistic when her daughter began to date and stay out late. She remembered her own troubled adolescence filled with sexual activity and drinking. "She'll be just like me," Fran lamented. Fran responded to her daughter's natural desire to go to parties and date with fear and heavy restrictions. Her daughter rebelled. Finally, with a close friend's help, Fran was able to see that her daughter was a different person and had grown up in a different family, a healthier family. She didn't have the same empty places in her heart that Fran had experienced as a teenager. When Fran began to work on her own psychological pain, her relationship with her daughter improved dramatically, and Fran began to set healthy, realistic limits.

How daughters differ from sons

Whereas we encourage our sons to separate and become autonomous, the ego boundaries between ourselves and our daughters are "more fluid, more undefined."[2] Even in infancy our daughters receive different responses from us. From the beginning, we look at and talk to our daughters more often than our sons.[3] And by thirteen months of age, our sons touch us less frequently, stay away from us longer, and venture further away than do our daughters. The results of psychological research show that we encourage separation, exploration, and autonomy in our sons while maintaining closer interpersonal ties with our daughters.

Of course, sons and daughters do not respond to us alike. Child development expert Eleanor Maccoby says that as early as ten months of age, boys are more insistent in their demands for their mother's attention. And if a mother withdraws her attention? A daughter will accept this, but sons will increase the intensity of their demands. They keep pushing until their mothers capitulate.

Throughout childhood, our daughters approach us in friendly, sociable ways, wanting us to help them or play with them. Sons, on the other hand, approach us with requests or even demands. Maccoby says that they tend to ask for "some form of service or attempt to control or dominate."[4] Consequently, we may find that we spend more time disciplining our sons than our daughters and therefore have more time to enjoy our girls.

But these often aggressive and dominating sons are not as tough as they seem. Sons are more psychologically vulnerable in the face of family discord than daughters.[5] But our daughters are particularly vulnerable in the areas of self-esteem and intimacy.

In 1926 Rose Wilder Lane, only child of the famed Laura Ingalls Wilder, wrote an article for *Cosmopolitan* entitled "I Discovered the Secret of Happiness on the Day I Tried to Kill Myself."[6] A writer who struggled with depression, Rose felt her mother was too busy, too anxious, too tired, and too hypercritical to give her the love, acceptance, and emotional support she craved. A friend said that Rose, who provided for her parents financially and launched her mother's writing career, "was very much her mama's slave."[7] And it was said of Rose, who spent years in Albania, that she loved her parents in direct proportion to her geographic distance from home.[8] So famed Laura Ingalls Wilder was not able to create with her own daughter the warm, familial relationship she wrote about in her books.

Gifts we give our daughters

This sometimes wonderful, sometimes frightening, unique relationship with our daughters begins in the womb. And once they are born, we nurture them and give them gifts that will shape their experiences for the rest of their lives.

One of the most powerful gifts we give our daughters is nurturance. Psychologist Juanita Williams defines nurturance as "a readiness to give care and comfort to others, especially to those whose condition manifests such a need: the young, the weak, and the sick."[9] With our children, this nurturance is an essential part of mother love that translates into consistent, sensitive, responsive mothering. It is that crazy-about-you kind of love that often puts their needs ahead of our own.

I tell my friend Anne Marie that if she could package the warmth and nurture she gives her family and friends, it would go for $100 a bottle. Anne Marie, who speaks lovingly of her own attractive mother, a fourth grade school teacher in her sixties, is fondly called by close friends "the Nurturer of the World."

To visit Anne Marie, whether for lunch or a weekend, is to be greeted warmly at the door and led into her living room to a comfy chair. Within minutes, coffee and a sumptuous dessert magically appear, and Anne Marie sits down, giving you her undivided attention. "Now tell me about your life," she says as she listens attentively. Full of laughter, Anne Marie is a busy, vital woman, but she gives her friends the feeling she has nothing better to do than relate to them.

And she has nurtured her own daughter well. Anne Marie's ten-year-old daughter Sarah exhibits those qualities psychologists say are the hallmarks of emotional security and high self-esteem. She is cooperative with adults, popular with peers, and achievement oriented. A happy girl, Sarah is comfortable with her femininity and greets the world, just like her mother, with an open, friendly gaze.

Another gift we give our daughters is allowing them to see us love their fathers well. As they watch us respect and honor our husbands, this teaches them how to relate to men. Susan Yates says, "My daughters not only learn how to be a woman from me, but they learn how to love their future husbands. They hear me bragging on Johnny and listen as I build him up. 'Your dad is so reliable; I can always count on him,' I tell them. 'He's rock-solid, dependable.'" She continues, "Of course, we're honest with the children about our weaknesses. But I feel one of the most important things any mother does for her daughter is to allow her to see the respect she has for her husband—that she watches her language and never cuts him down."

All our children flourish if we have happy, satisfying marriages. All are hurt in their souls when we don't. The answer? We need to work on our marriages for ourselves and for our children.

We train our daughters for motherhood

Not only do we teach our daughters powerful lessons about love and nurture when we respond to their cries, pick them up, talk to them, and hold them, but we train them for motherhood as we engage in everyday activities of life—shopping, cooking, talking. Anne Marie says her mother taught her that "motherhood was the highest calling a woman could have. Not that this was the only important thing a woman did with her life, mind you. But that it was a rich and wonderful calling. My mother lived a full life, but she always gave me the sense that she *enjoyed* me. And that's made an enormous difference in my life."

If we value our human connections above all else and put our family's needs first, our daughters will probably do the same. If we feel that caring for children—for them—is menial, unfulfilling, and boring work, they may come to share those beliefs as well. Unfortunately, in our culture for the past thirty years we have denigrated mothering and nurturance while pushing our daughters into the arena of achievement. In fact, many women have told me they get more flak from their mothers than anyone else if they take a season out of their professional lives to nurture their children.

An article in the *Wall Street Journal* (April 28, 1994) by William R. Mattox, Jr., vice president for policy at the Family Research Council in Washington, D.C., beautifully illustrates one mother's gift of nurture to her child.

◆ ◆ ◆

A Lesson for Allison

I am not the kind of guy who normally takes part in feminist "consciousness-raising" efforts. But I am participating in Take Your Daughter to Work Day today because I have an eight-year-old daughter whose self-esteem matters a great deal to me.

For the uninitiated, Take Your Daughter to Work Day is an annual event dreamed up by the Ms. Foundation in response to research showing that girls' self-esteem often plummets during the fragile pre-teen and early adolescent years. By exposing young girls to successful women in the workplace, organizers hope that girls will learn to think more highly of females in general and of themselves in particular.

I have a great day planned for my daughter, Allison. This morning, I plan to take her by the offices of two women whose job it is to meet regularly with members of Congress and other public officials. Then, I plan to have her talk with a young woman who just finished graduate school at Johns Hopkins University and is now serving as a health policy analyst. At lunch, she'll chat with a woman who does some public speaking, and another who crunches numbers in our accounting department. Finally, in the late afternoon, Allison is scheduled to meet with a woman who used to practice law and now manages a bevy of staff writers.

I am sure all of this will be interesting to Allison. But the time I am most looking forward to is the ride home. For it is then that I plan to point out to my daughter that some of the exciting tasks carried out by my female colleagues in the workplace are tasks my wife performed in jobs she held prior to motherhood. She used to meet regularly with congressmen and senators. She used to do some writing and public speaking. And she has a Phi Beta Kappa key from her college days.

After I remind my daughter of these things, I plan to turn to her and look her in the eye and say, "Allison, you must be a very special young girl. Your mother could be using her talents and skills in all sorts of jobs in the workplace, but she has chosen instead to use them at home teaching you. She must love you very, very much and think you are very, very important."

Somehow, I think that at that moment my daughter's self-esteem will rise to a level heretofore unimagined by the organizers of Take Your Daughter to Work Day. And for that I owe a debt of gratitude to my wife, whose esteem-building job as a mother at home rarely receives the public esteem it deserves.[10]

Through giving we heal ourselves

The act of mothering our daughters can in itself be healing for our childhood wounds. In her book *Mothers and Daughters* Edith Neisser says, "So much does a woman feel herself a part of her daughter that, as she gives to her, she is compensating herself for those deficiencies in affection or encouragement or independence or whatever it may have been, that plagued her own childhood."[11]

According to the late psychoanalyst Selma Fraiberg, what is central is that parents remember the *feelings* from their own injured childhood, not just the facts.[12] In other words, as we remember our longings, sadnesses, and unmet needs, we can work to keep from doing to our children what was done to us. But the mother who simply remembers the facts of a painful childhood is still cut off from her feelings and will likely perpetuate the pain.

So while it is hard psychological work, our daughters give us the opportunity and the challenge to rework old psychological issues and to find emotional healing from our childhood wounds.

We stay tethered by their love

One of the great rewards of being emotionally close to our daughters throughout their years at home is the comfort of knowing that they are bound to us by an invisible, incredibly strong tether—a cord of love and positive regard. And this cord draws our daughters back to us across the years. Suzanne makes a yearly trek to her family's lake cottage in the Midwest to spend three weeks each summer with her mother. While her husband and father join the women for one week, Suzanne and her mother value their two weeks alone together. "No matter which part of the country I live in, or what other vacations my husband and I take, I protect that time with my mom. It means a great deal to both of us."

Mothers need their daughters as much as daughters need their mothers That invisible tether gives a mother peace of mind, and it gives her daughter confidence in her mother's love. Just recently my daughter Kristen and a friend had a conversation about their mothers in which Kristen said matter-of-factly, "I know my mother would die for me." When I heard about the conversation, I thought about Kristen's calm assurance and wondered, "Would I die for my daughters?" Coward though I am, my love for my daughters is so intense and so foundational I can conceive of making this ultimate sacrifice.

A friend of mine recently appeared on the Leeza Show opposite a psychologist and three other mothers torn between their careers and their desire to be good mothers. My friend was asked to be a guest because she, a mother at home, was "passionate about mothering." On the show, the psychologist dismissed my friend's statements about the importance of mothering, saying her testimony was "anecdotal evidence at best and thus didn't really count." After all, she was only a mother and not a psychologist.

After the show, the psychologist, her thirteen-year-old daughter, and my friend boarded the same plane to fly back east. As the women rushed to change flights at O'Hare Airport in Chicago, the child's face turned white. My friend handed her an empty paper bag. The child begin to throw up, but the psychologist, scarcely seeming to notice, took off at a dead run to catch her connecting flight. Her daughter was left to trail after her, continuing to retch into the bag.

As my friend settled into her seat bound for Washington, D.C., she, who had been verbally assailed on national television for saying that motherhood is a sophisticated, one-on-one profession, was comforted by her priorities. She flew home to spend time with a daughter whose needs sometimes come before her own, a daughter who, at six, is confident she is deeply loved by her mother.

It matters to our daughters that we are passionately committed to mothering and that we are crazy about them. It matters that they internalize the message that their emotional and spiritual needs are more important to us than our careers, our connecting flights, or the perennial housework which demands our attention. It matters that our daughters have a harmonious relationship with us in order to feel good about themselves.

So how can we protect these lifelines?

It is never too late for a mother to go to her daughter and ask that they work together to improve their relationship. If a mother can pack up her pride, dismantle some of her defenses, and reach out to her daughter lovingly, the daughter may respond with forgiveness and grace. I've seen this happen in my office as I have worked with daughters and their mothers to overcome the past and deepen their emotional bonds. I have watched the daughter's self-esteem soar once she became good friends with her mother. Moreover, I've experienced the healing of the mother/daughter relationship in my own life.

◆　◆　◆

Last night after a party Holly and I curled up on the sofa in the family room and had a warm, happy conversation. She, wired from her success as a hostess, and I, in full flight from this book, needed some debriefing time. As I looked at my blond daughter, I remembered the healing that had come several years earlier in our relationship.

Holly reluctantly moved back home after college and occupied the guest suite in our old Virginia farmhouse. She hadn't wanted to come home, but she hadn't made other plans. Her close friends had moved away—Terenia to graduate school in Virginia and Alison to the Caribbean. While Holly had been accepted to graduate school, she didn't really want to go.

So home she came to find a new job and a new set of friends. About this time Don began to negotiate a contract in St. Louis and spent the better part of four months there, leaving Holly and me to spend many evenings together, talking over coffee. It was during this time that my relationship with my daughter began to change.

I had always loved Holly dearly but knew she had suffered greatly as a result of the divorce. When her daddy left, she was three and her heart was broken. She was the little girl who rode on his shoulders and ran to meet him each night. In truth, Holly was closer to David than to me. A year after he left, I gave up a teaching job, sold our house and car, and moved the three of us to London in search of Christian community. Holly still remembers the sorrow she felt in going to my junior English class to give away her kittens.

So Holly's early life was punctuated with losses: father, home, kittens. Symbols of security and continuity. She and her sister also missed out on a lot of mothering. I was depressed that first year after David left and had little to give Kristen or Holly. I also worked full-time during their infancies. It wasn't until we three moved to London that I was better able to care for the emotional needs of my children.

How did the tears of her early life affect Holly? Outwardly, she was cheerful, compliant, sometimes buried in books. She was the responsible elder daughter who excelled in school and was the only girl from her school selected to attend the state Governor's School for the Gifted. Inwardly, she struggled with low self-esteem and self-doubt.

As for our relationship, it grew strained during college. She dressed in funeral black and second-hand men's blazers. Fortunately, Holly's rebellion stayed superficial. But she was distant. This was not just freewheeling, happy independence; there was a sense of desperation in the short stories she got As on, stories about parents who didn't understand and who exacted too high a price for their love, stories about the high cost of divorce.

During this post-college period when we lived together, Holly recounted some painful childhood memories. She cried. I put my arms around her, told her I loved her, and prayed that God would mend my lovely, sad daughter. Holly spoke of David, of feelings of rejection. She spoke of my perfectionism and the sense that my love for her was based on her performance. "Would you love me if I failed?" my beautiful daughter wailed, and I was pierced to the heart.

"Of course, of course," I said, burdened by the pain her father and I had bequeathed her. I asked Holly's forgiveness for not having given her the stability and nurture her heart had craved, and she forgave me. Soon my daughter started to grow stronger. As she became more confident of my love, her self-image improved and her self-doubt evaporated. She took more risks—traveling alone in Europe for three months, confronting her father face-to-face, and talking candidly to her stepmother.

At twenty-seven, Holly has come into her own. Don says she has never been lovelier or more confident. She is matter-of-fact about her parents, their strengths and shortcomings. Holly has rich friendships and is an ace negotiator at getting raises. Recently, she moved into a condo that she purchased with her own money, and she is basking in the experience of living in her colorful habitat. (She painted the living room a warm watermelon red.)

Best of all, Holly has a sense of belonging—to me, to Don, to herself—that she once lacked.

What has healing our relationship meant to me? I feel free from worry, longing, fear for my child. I don't believe any mother who's estranged from her daughter rests easy or sleeps soundly at night. Besides, because both my daughters now feel secure in my love, I can feel confident that their children will experience a legacy of emotional security and mother love that they were denied.

And folks, that's about as good as it gets.

7

• • •

The Sister Knot

Nobody's seen the trouble I've seen but you.

Adrienne Rich, *"Leaflets"*

My husband, an only child, does not understand my relationship with my sister. He is often baffled by the tenacity of our sister knot and the depth of the pain I feel when we are estranged. My sister's husband, also an only child, watches in wonderment as Sandy and I live out our sister drama, sometimes close and supportive, sometimes wounding. I think that if our husbands formed a two-person support group, they would better understand the relationship that Sandy and I, in our fifties, are finally viewing with increasing objectivity.

The four of us are not alone in our failure to understand the paradoxes inherent in sisterhood. In her book *The Sister Bond*, Toni A. H. McNaron says, "The relationship between sisters, like that between mothers and daughters, comes to us shrouded in silence and ignorance."[1] Although researchers have paid scant attention to this relationship, our sisters are powerful figures in our lives. We love them. We compete with them. While we applaud their successes, we secretly hope they will not receive more from life than we have—more success, more love, more. As children, we kept score, and as we grew, we monitored our sisters' progress. Said one older sister in her late twenties, "My sister was a basketball star in high school. I wasn't. And in college she caught up with me academically. I want to outstrip her just once."

We don't like to admit that this relationship is flawed by competitive feelings. Sometimes jealousy and competition are muted, if sisters are far apart in age or if their parents are fair in the distribution of goods and praise. Usually, however, we have to deny our competitive feelings to stay connected.

Sisters share the same reality

A sister not only possesses the same set of parents, grew up in the same family, and knows the same relatives, but most important, she witnessed many of the same events we did. Liza, a single woman in her forties, says that her sister Annabeth understands her better than anyone. "We grew up in the same house and attended the same college. She knows my parents. She was the one who hopped in the car with me at midnight to go to the hospital when our mother was ill." She adds, "I go to her home for the holidays. My sister provides a lot of security."

Our sisters share the same reality; they, like us, are the family historians, particularly when it comes to relationships. They shed critical light on the intricacies of our family web.

When a client comes to my office and says she wants to understand her distant or rejecting mother better, I may send her to her mother's sister. This aunt has valuable information in her memory bank if she is perceptive. She can tell my client about her mother's emotional connection to her own mother and about her mother's girlhood, dating experiences, self-esteem, and friendships.

One woman who had trouble understanding why her mother-in-law, Grace, was so cold and unfriendly, visited Grace's elder sister. She learned that Grace had been confined at home with her aging parents. Denied normal friendships, she spent a lonely adolescence on their Iowa farm. Grace was particularly angry at her mother, and this affected her relationship with her sister and later her daughter-in-law. Although Grace continued to be hostile and distant, her daughter-in-law changed her perceptions about the older woman. In learning about Grace's girlhood, she was better able to treat her with understanding and compassion.

They are our expanded selves

Not only do our sisters share our early reality, they are also our "expanded selves." McNaron writes, "A sister can be seen as someone who is both ourselves and very much not ourselves—a special kind of double."[2]

Literary greats Virginia Woolf and Christina Rosetti both saw their sisters as extensions of themselves.[3] Virginia Woolf, childless in her marriage to Leonard because of her husband's "distaste for fatherhood," satisfied her maternal longings through her sister Vanessa's brood. "She seems to have been a model parent to her nephews and niece whenever Vanessa left for the sunnier climes of Italy."[4]

Just as Virginia Woolf looked to her sister for something her life lacked, so did the British poet Christina Rosetti. Christina's sister Maria possessed a deeper piety and more cheerful disposition than did her creative sister. "In both her poetry and prose…Christina praised Maria and recognized that without her sister's example, her own depression and defiance would have poisoned her work and her life."[5] In sum, Christina's close relationship with her sister provided the optimism, stability, and "balance" her own life lacked.

When Christina began writing poetry at age eleven, Maria, who had better penmanship, copied the final versions of the poems. Later when Maria faced death with joy and "rapture," she gave her sister some of her hope and confidence in the goodness of God. Years after Maria died, Christina described her as her "irreplaceable sister and friend."[6]

Sisters as best friends

When sisters are emotionally close, they provide a component often lacking in other female friendships—practical help. For example, a woman will often look to her sister for advice, emotional support, and help with the day-to-day demands of living, especially if her husband is not particularly involved in child rearing.[7]

This fall when their eighty-six-year-old mother, Ilde, had hip surgery followed a month later by surgery for lung cancer, Eleanor and her younger sister, Anne, were a tight, supportive unit. On the day Ilde had her second operation the sisters waited together for hours at a northern Virginia hospital, along with their two aunts. During the long days of their mother's convalescence, the sisters talked daily on the phone. And when Ilde had to be re-admitted into intensive care, Anne drove the five hours from her home in New Jersey posthaste. Later Idle told her daughters she would not have made it through the surgeries without their love and care.

Anne and Eleanor were able to link arms to care for their mother this fall because they have been an integral part of each other's lives for years. They have summer cottages at a camp that has been in the family since they were children. Together they celebrate the high points of life and most holidays. They have become each other's good friends.

Sisters may even parent each other

My sister is an irreplaceable and integral part of my life. When Sandy and I were very young, I used to say I was the city mouse and she was the country mouse. I grew up in several small southern cities; Sandy lived on a dairy farm, attended country schools, and seldom visited public libraries or museums. Only during summers or Christmases did we share the same reality. I left the South to attend college; she married after she graduated from high school. Because my sister and I grew up apart, I have had little difficulty seeing my sister as different from me. Yet we are amazingly similar in values and perceptions. Moreover, Sandy is an intelligent and wise, wise woman. And she and I visit rooms of our past that only we have inhabited. At such moments we are more like an "expanded self."

In a real sense, Sandy alone shared all of my early hopes, fears, and longings. Neither of us talked in-depth to our mother, who when I was five took me to live with her and left Sandy to be reared by Granny and Granddaddy. Because of our early losses, Sandy and I turned to each other for comfort and nurture.

As young children, we created rooms among the sugar cane and chased baby ducks. One summer's day we lay on the ground, clad only in our underpants, scanning the clouds for our dead father's face. "I see him," I told Sandy, pointing to a cloud formation. "I see him too," she said. I was the older sister, the leader. She was the follower and my echo.

This gave me a sense of responsibility for her welfare, but it also gave me a power I misused on occasion. One Christmas I blatantly lied to her. Looking out the window beside our bed, I, who no longer believed in Santa, said to Sandy, "I just saw Santa and his reindeer." "Where? Where?" asked my sister, struggling across the covers to peer out the window. "He's gone," I said. "Oh tell me about him," begged Sandy. And I wove a wonderful, magical story that she believed.

Sandy not only believed my stories, she believed in me. I, a street child, who was growing up spending too many hours alone, needed that. And I? I nurtured her as I taught her the multiplication tables (long after Granddaddy had given up) and shared my faith in God as well as my moral values. "You taught me about sexual morality," says my sister who needed better parenting than she received during her adolescence when our grandparents were in their sixties, too tired to lock horns with a teenager.

As adults, Sandy and I have come to see that we were not only siblings reared in separate households, but we were cast in the parental role in each other's lives. Being two years older, I usually filled the mothering role, but Sandy on occasion stood in the parent gap for me. She helped me trek hot dusty roads one summer to sell newspaper subscriptions to pay for majorette camp. The night I came in second in the local beauty pageant which offered a five hundred dollar college scholarship, only Sandy was backstage to comfort me.

The fact that we were parents to each other as well as siblings has created the greatest pain for us in adulthood. It means that occasionally our expectations for each other are just too high, especially at those perilous times in life—the graduations, weddings, celebrations—when parents typically stand in the gap. At such times, we cannot be simply sisters, but we unconsciously expect the other to play the role of mother as well. Invariably we end up being disappointed.

While Sandy and I were psychological orphans, some sisters struggle with literal orphanhood. In her book *Orphans*, psychotherapist Eileen

Simpson writes about how the death of her mother left her and her sister Marie greatly dependent upon each other. This was evident when Eileen was having difficulty recovering from an operation. Finally, her father realized that Eileen's separation from Marie might be prolonging her sickness, and he convinced the doctors that Marie should be allowed to come to the hospital for an extended visit. Eileen, who had thought her sister was dead, was delighted. She later said, "From my response to her seeming resurrection, and the spurt my convalescence took, there could be little doubt that he (my father) had been right."[8]

Why some sisters aren't close

Most sisters, however, don't grow up so psychologically dependent on each other. In fact, some studies indicate that only 40 percent of women are very close to their sisters and perhaps as few as 20 percent view them as best friends.[9] In sum, while some women view their sisters as bosom buddies, the majority do not.

As a psychologist, I have wondered why some sisters are emotionally close while others are coolly distant or even engage in open conflict, and I have come to believe that the mother is key in the formation of the sister bond. "My mother taught us to be close," says my friend Jennifer Leber. "I remember the first birthday party I attended when I was six. Julie, then four, wasn't invited, and I can still see her unhappy little face pressed against the window as she waved good-bye. My mother handled this situation beautifully. She not only told me to bring a special surprise back for Julie, but she said to Julie, 'I know you feel sad, but each of you needs to have your own set of friends.' My mother helped us see each other as a separate being."

Over the years Jennifer's mom patiently instructed both girls in the art of sisterhood. "She taught each of us to be the other's cheerleader," said Jennifer. "When I got an award, my mother taught Julie to be happy for me because her time would come. And it did."

Jennifer's story underscores the important role a mother has in teaching her children to be close. In working with my daughters I've tried to downplay sibling rivalry by affirming each girl's gifts as well as her differences.

Though the girls had different interests and personality types, I made sure they had time to play without interruption, believing that playing together helped create a bond. As children, they played together for hours on end, and their doll games are legendary. Holly used to make shoe box houses, curtains, and tiny furniture for their dolls, while Kristen watched, transfixed. One Christmas Day they played behind closed doors for eight hours, only staggering out of their bedroom to go to the bathroom and eat Christmas dinner.

Interestingly, the research shows that friendship between sisters ebbs and flows across the life cycle. Sisters are most often close as children, more distant as young adults, but often find each other again as they mature and move into midlife and beyond.[10]

This parallels the development of our friendships with other females. We forge those close bonds as children and teenagers. Then in our twenties and early thirties, when we are finding a mate or establishing a career, friendships may be put on the back burner. As we hit our mid thirties and settle into our single or married life, we establish close female bonds with a new urgency. And in midlife, our friends and sisters take on even more importance.

Sisters in midlife

Recently I attended Rachel's forty-fifth birthday party for which she had asked six of her closest friends to dinner. Her invitation read: "Please don't bring me a personal gift. I'd like you to bring instead the gift of words of wisdom written down on paper for me to keep. Share something of what God has taught you over the years that you think will encourage me as I look to the future and 'finish the course.'

Rachel's friends gathered on that cold, crisp Sunday afternoon, and a special guest drove five hours from North Carolina: her sister Nancy. Rachel was delighted that Nancy, a mother and social worker, had cared enough to come. Nancy was the last to speak, and as she described her love for Rachel, she started to cry. At the other end of the table, Rachel listened, her face also glistening with tears.

What made the moment especially meaningful was the letter Nancy had written to Rachel as a nine-year-old on the day Rachel had left for Girl

Scout camp. This letter, now more than thirty years old, was propped up at Rachel's plate.

July 20, 1959

Dear Rachel,

I know you'll laugh at this letter. I am a little lonesome for you. I wish I could have stayed [at camp] with you. Please write me. I don't really like to fuss with you. Now I am sore [sic] of sorry I said I was glad you were leaving.

Love,
Nancy

P.S. Please forgive me for all the times I've been mean to you.

That childhood letter and the birthday celebration many years later attest to the enduring quality of the sister knot. Our sisters never cease to be important to us. They share our genetic legacy and, as Nancy said to Rachel, some part of the reality that was our first family.

And if we become estranged from them because of unresolved anger? Toni A. H. McNaron says that when this happens, sisters experience great pain and longing, "a sense of having been split from themselves violently, inexplicably."[11] "Even when one sister senses that resolution will not be forthcoming, they struggle to figure out the fight, to work out the damage, go on until something changes and some peace is achieved."[12]

Amy, twenty-five, speaks of a distant and painful relationship with her older sister Carrie:

I almost never see my sister. She lives five minutes away and I have less contact with her than with the office cleaning staff. This deeply hurts me, but I feel I have no choice. When I have tried to jump-start our relationship, I have had my emotions bashed. Only when Carrie is in a period of intense need (post-college and needing to meet a new social set, moody after a bitter break-up) has she turned to me. Briefly. Naturally, this has made me cynical. Right now there is a window of opportunity for us, a window I hold open despite the numbness I feel inside and out. But I cannot hold it open indefinitely. Maybe someday she'll turn to me, but years are a long time to wait. I can learn to be selfish too.

Amy's words reveal the angst that comes when sisters are estranged. Until Amy and Carrie work through their relationship, each will always be on the periphery of the other's mind—a painful shadow that needs to be dealt with.

Many of us would say we need a harmonious relationship with our sisters to feel good about ourselves and about life. We may not be as close to our sisters as Mae is—who at ninety hears from each of her five sisters daily—but we need to be at peace with them. If we are, we provide positive modeling for our daughters and greater opportunity for extended family gatherings.

As part of achieving this rapprochement, we may need to release our sisters from our expectations and accept what they are able to give us, be it little or much. If they give little, we have to find what we need in our friends. And, in the process, turn our friends into sisters.

Turning friends into sisters

One woman who was continually disappointed by her sister was comforted by a wise and perceptive friend: "You may never find what you long for in your sister. But if you look at all your relationships with your friends, you'll find you have many friend-sisters. God has met your need to be close to other women even though your sister isn't interested in a relationship right now."

It is possible to turn friends into sisters who will be our confidantes, attend life's important celebrations with us, and offer practical help that our sisters, because of physical or psychological distance, may not be able to provide. The day I defended my dissertation before the psychology faculty at Georgetown, I was almost paralyzed with anxiety. As I walked into the conference room, I saw my friend Sherry, sitting cross-legged on a table. "Hello, Brenda," she said. "I hope you know I love you since I got up at five in the morning to drive five hours to get here." Sherry was joined by Linda and Eleanor, along with Chap, my friend and statistician who had worked magic with numbers and helped me immensely. They, along with Don, Holly, and Kristen provided emotional support, and that night all came to the party my thoughtful husband gave for me.

Sisters. These women share our genetic legacy; they and we are, as poet Christina Rosetti said, "two blossoms on one stem." And just as some universal law dictates that we remain connected to our parents, so some inner rule states that we need to nurture the sister bond, for we need these "expanded selves" our whole life long.

◆　◆　◆

Sisters

My sister and I have been entangled from the womb, but not because we shared it at the same time. She occupied it first. Ever since, the message has been clear: first come, first served. This message was summarized well in a birthday card she recently gave me: "Happy Birthday to my Sister the Princess," it says on the outside. On the inside: "From her Sister the Queen."

Sandy and I grew from the same bone house, from the same mother's soul. Maybe that's why it gets so confusing. Hers was one of the first faces looming over my crib and she stuck more than fingers in between the bars, poking, probing, reminding me that I would never outshine her, never have a shadow as large as hers. Her goal, it seemed, was to keep me measuring just how large that shadow was.

Once when I was about eleven years old and triumphantly mowing the half-acre front yard with a hand mower, Sandy arrived on the scene. I said rather proudly, "Look, I did this all by myself. I'm almost finished." Four years older than me, and certainly wiser, she said: "Can I just push the mower a little bit?" "Okay," I said.

She struggled with the twirling metal beast no more than six feet, turned to me, unclutched the handle, and slapped her hands together. Just before running off she announced, "Now you can't say you did it all by yourself."

Of course there were other times, some funny, some not, humiliation being the modus operandi. When I wanted an old purse of hers, she demanded, "Only if you kiss my feet." Barefoot, her feet neither smelled nor looked so good. Reptilian is the closest adjective I could come up with. Being an animal lover, however, I suffered the agony of bending to her feet, only to have her change her mind.

We got older. I grew breasts larger and sooner than she. That pretty much finished us. Jealousy raged, although I didn't understand this until an adult. Now as a thirty-eight-year-old woman I've come to believe sisters are born with an innate competitiveness that both drives and melds us simultaneously. Our relationship is fraught with conflict, but beneath the prize of mother and father and siblings, beyond measuring the shadow, there's something deeper. Something that's taken me decades to grasp. She's my best friend.

At forty-two, Sandy insists we are twins when we meet strangers or when I am introduced to her friends. I squirm; she beams. The truth is we do look alike, but can't they see all those wrinkles around her eyes? The less defined jaw line? I claim I am younger and laugh. I say, "I'm the newer, improved version." She gets red, mad, silent. She's never admitted she's been wrong, at least when it comes to me.

Now we each have daughters the same age. Yesterday they and their friends gathered for a game of hide-and-seek. At one point, a friend of my niece's was asked where my daughter was. She answered, "Oh, we didn't bother finding her." It seems some things get carried on.

As adults, there's no one like a sister to remind you of who you once were, what your foibles are, what history you hail from, and most of all, what mistakes and sins you've committed. But she's there, a few houses away from me. Maybe if we lived a few states apart instead, the relationship might be less intense. No matter what the distance, I know she's there; we can't escape each other. We don't want to.

Underlying our history from the womb on, a belief in each other surfaces despite the conflicts. There's little more powerful than that belief. She knows who I am. She's been there since my beginning. She'll always be there. We share a language only families understand: a heart kind of Braille. Touching, knowing, supporting.

I've come to understand that in my sister's shadow there is shade for me. In her, I've found a lifetime companion.

Sherry Von Ohlsen is a writer and single mother who hails from Sparta, New Jersey. A journalist, she has published more than eighty articles in the Christian Science Monitor, Bride *magazine and* The World and I, *among others. She has two daughters, Lindsay, eleven, and Erin, sixteen.*

8

• • •

Women and Friendship

Few comforts are more alluring for a woman than the rich intimate territory of women's talk.... A woman friend will say, "You are not alone. I have felt that way, too. This is what happened to me." Home, in other words.

Elsa Walsh, Washington Post reporter

"Jenise has more friends than anyone I know," says Kathryn, a longtime friend. "She keeps up with everyone: former coworkers, roommates, high school and college friends, and people in her college internship program. She even has friends from first grade!" Who is this young woman? And why is she so adept at making and keeping friends?

By her own admission, Jenise, a single, attractive twenty-nine-year-old who sells legal publishing products, works hard at friendship. "I try to maintain some presence in my friends' lives. I write them notes telling them how much they mean to me, or I call them fairly often. Sometimes I make financial sacrifices to see them, like when I flew to Oregon recently. I value friendship above just about anything."

Friendship is essential

Friendship is one of the things women do best. We are better at making friends than many of the things we put our minds to because it comes naturally. Among the women I interviewed, many felt better about their

109

female friendships than their relationships with their mothers, daughters, or sometimes, unfortunately, even their husbands.

Why is this true? Our family relationships require work. We sometimes struggle to be the responsive mother, the dutiful daughter, and the intimate wife. Most of us have a hard time keeping all the relational balls we juggle in the air. But when it comes to our friends, we can generally relax. Friends are the support players who usually require fewer emotional supplies than family members and who help us with our problems.

Our friends are important for our everyday survival. Said one woman of her female friends: "If I didn't have my friends around me, I couldn't exist. You love your family, you love all of them, but it's just something you have to have and without it, life's not complete."[1]

Most women would agree. Our friends are among our life's greatest treasures. They help us negotiate the difficult hurdles of life. What would we have done without friends in adolescence to help us navigate the travails of puberty and deal with our "unreasonable" parents? And what about our twentysomething romances? Whom do we go to for emotional rescue when in the dating years the man of our dreams becomes the stuff of nightmares? We go to our friends. Later, they coach us through first-time motherhood. Years later as we help our kids pack for college, they witness our tears. Our friends walk with us through menopause as, once again, we are caught up in the hormonal crazies, and they listen as we fantasize about fleeing to the Caribbean or a convent.

In their presence, we laugh about what drove us crazy hours before; with them we cry without shame, knowing we will be understood.

Women are better at friendship than men

In *Worlds of Friendship*, sociologist Robert Bell states that women have more friendships than men their whole life long and their friendships are deeper.[2] He observes that women disclose more than men and their friendships are richer in spontaneity and confidences.[3]

Psychologist Joel Block agrees. In *Friendship: How to Give It, How to Get It*, Block says that though the friendships of men "have been sung about and celebrated across the ages," in reality most men are not close to other men.[4] Forget David and Jonathan, Achilles and Patroclus, Butch Cassidy and the Sundance Kid! In Block's research, 84 percent said they would not "dare" to be open with other men. Block writes, "Upon being interviewed about their comrades, men frequently spoke of distrust and only occasionally of loyalty.... Having learned caution, they expected neither sympathy nor devotion from their brothers. On the contrary, their experiences are filled with incidents of rivalry and betrayal."[5]

Expecting betrayal, men "shy away from intimacy," particularly in the sexual area. Block found that only eight out of a hundred would risk having a frank discussion about their sex life with a comrade.[6] Personal ambition is an even more taboo topic among men. Block says, "In-depth interviews reveal that becoming competent and well-respected in an occupation weighs heavily on the male soul."[7] Whereas women love to hear other women talk about their weaknesses and vulnerabilities, Block says that most men never disclose their weaknesses for fear of attack.[8]

And when they feel they must speak from the heart? Typically both men and women confide in other women. In fact, one study indicated that both men and women have their deepest and most rewarding relationships with women.[9] Women, then, are the intimacy experts for both sexes.

We do different things when we are together than men do with other men. Our relationships are based on intimacy rather than shared activities. We love to talk, visit, be together. Men prefer to do things together: watch TV, play basketball, fish. Jennifer laughs when she recounts a visit she and her husband made to long-time friends recently. "We hadn't seen these friends for months, but while I was in the kitchen asking Cindy intimate details about her life—just renewing our friendship—our husbands, who are also good friends, were at the computer, talking about different programs. Isn't that something! The sexes really are different."

Women are the bane of any waiter's existence. When we're out for a meal, we talk and talk. Hours go by. Other tables fill up and empty as the waiter circles endlessly. "Be sure you tip generously," says my daughter Holly, who used to waitress in college. "You are killing the waiter's tips."

I'm not alone in spending hours confiding in friends. Other women also tell their female friends about their personal and family problems, their hopes, fears, and dreams. And what relief it brings us to share our feelings openly with a compassionate friend.

Women "do" friendship unconsciously

Although women are generally good at it, many women "do" friendship at an unconscious level. While I was interviewing women for this book, some struggled to articulate their views on friendship. Their responses were frequently vague or general. Said one woman, "You're making me think about something I've apparently done all my life; I've always had lots of friends. But I've never really thought a lot about friendship per se." This is not to say that women don't think a lot about their *friends*, but rather that they rarely analyze their *friendships*.

How many of us think consciously about levels of friendship—that is, how many close friends and acquaintances we currently have in our friendship bank? How many of us have a carefully thought-out plan for handling conflict? Few of us indeed, which leaves most of us waltzing away from conflict with our female friends.

Women's friendships have been trivialized

Perhaps the fact we don't think much about our friendships as a subject for discourse is because, historically, both men and women have trivialized and devalued women's friendships. Robert Bell notes that social scientists have treated women's friendships as unimportant and peripheral and this trivialization has reinforced women's dependency on men.[10]

Joel Block believes that not only have women's friendship bonds been treated as inferior to men's but that history views female friendships as treacherous. Block says, "Competing for men, from which they derive their identity, they are depicted as fiercely—albeit subtly—rivalrous toward one another."[11] Sebastian Chamfort, an eighteenth century writer, would agree. He said, "However bad the things a man may think about women, there is no woman who does not think worse of them than he."[12]

While no woman will deny the rivalrous, competitive feelings that can exist in female friendships, these do not destroy the enormous value women have in each other's lives. Just as no heterosexual friendship is without its problems, so no female friendship is completely without rivalry. But most women can handle that tension and, in fact, may deal with the rivalry openly and with humor. Two women in their fifties were walking to the parking lot after having lunch out. Their respective cars—an emerald green, 1993 Jaguar and a faded, 1986 Chevy with dented fender—were parked side by side. The owner of the Chevy looked at her car and then at her friend's and said, "Now, honestly, which one of us do you think God loves the best?"

A cultural aside

In spite of their innate competitiveness, women need each other in the nineties as never before. Not only has history trivialized female friendships, but during the last three decades we have glorified heterosexual relationships above all else. We have so sexualized relationships between men and women that we have created a stand-off between the sexes.

One blustery February night I spoke to three hundred Washington, D.C., singles on the subject of intimacy. As I packed up my papers to leave, a line formed in front of me. To my surprise, it was exclusively male. I remembered what John, the leader of "First Monday," had said when he asked me to speak: "There will be a lot of hurting people in the room. Many are divorced. Some have had multiple sexual relationships. Most long to be close to others, but they have been burned."

For more than an hour I listened to these men tell me about their pain, about the seemingly unbridgeable gap between the sexes, about their inability to develop enduring relationships with women. One of them who had three relationships end badly said, "I am not good at relationships." Some admitted that for the time being they had declared a moratorium on dating and searching for close heterosexual relationships.

As I left that night, I thought a lot about the "new eunuchs" created by the sexual revolution of the past three decades. And I realized that women, especially those who are single, need other women as never before. Emancipated from their families, they come home to empty apartments at night. Who will help them deal with loneliness? And when relationships end, to whom will they go for comfort?

We need our friends, whether single or married. Most of us know this and have between one and three best friends to count on. The *New Woman* survey found that 85 percent of the women polled have a "soul mate" and in nine out of ten cases that soul mate is another woman. In fact, most women polled said they communicate better with a female best friend (62 percent) than with a husband (51 percent). Apparently, our husbands give us love and support, but our best friendships give us that "open and easy relationship" we crave.

When asked to describe this best friend, the majority of women in the survey said, "She reads my mind." Seventy-two percent kept either no or few secrets from her. Says Lenore, one of the respondents, of her best friend: "I know her better than her husband does. There's very little we can't say to each other. Our relationship is based on a sense of trust and years of maturing together. We share the good and the bad. We party together, play together, go to movies, eat dinner together. And in psychological emergencies, we're there for each other."[13]

Our best friends are essential indeed.

Buffers against stress

Our friends, especially our best friends, are buffers against stress. They listen to our problems and concerns, and when we leave their presence, we feel better than we came. Is it little wonder that isolation depresses us and the company of our dearest friends relaxes and restores us? Sociologist Pat O'Connor says that women who are rich in friendships enjoy better physical health, live longer, and are less prone to alcoholism, suicide, and mental illness than those who are lonely and isolated.[14] Moreover, if we have close friends we see at least every two to three weeks, we can better handle the stresses of life's transitions: unemployment, divorce, and death of a family member.[15]

Friendships improve marriages

Married women need to be close to their husbands and a female friend. Studies have found that women who have close friends are happier in their marriages.[16] This is easy to understand. If we have friends we can talk to about our problems, we put less pressure on our husbands. We spread our needs around, and we get both a male and female perspective on our difficulties.

Many husbands understand that their wives need relationships with other women. Says Stan, "Vera's close friends take the pressure off me to provide all her emotional needs." Some men may initially be threatened when their wives spend a lot of time with friends ("She and her buddy talk about me," whines Henry). But over time most husbands find that their wives are happier when they also have close friends to confide in.

My husband has. Don says, "You're never happier than on those days you've spent time with other women." I find that if I have an argument with Don in the morning, and a heart-to-heart talk with a close friend before noon, by the time Don comes home from work, I am ready to see his point of view and work on our disagreements. He understands that I've aired my grievances—without character assassination—to my friend, we've laughed, and she has gently helped me see the problem from my husband's perspective. He isn't threatened by this at all but, rather, is relieved that I'm more amenable to his perspective.

Men may not know it, but their marriages have often been helped by their wife's best friend. Contrary to male fears, our best friends, even if they are privy to some of our marital issues, are not usually divisive. Following some rough marital weather, one woman talked about her best friend, Ann: "Jim has no idea how much of a debt he owes Ann. There have been days I wanted to leave him, even planned to leave him. But she urged me to work on my marriage. Some days she gave me hope when I felt pretty hopeless. I'm glad I didn't get a divorce because my marriage is working now, but I'm not sure I'd be married today if it hadn't been for Ann."

The ingredients of friendship

What's so special about women's friendships that they improve our mental health and buttress our marriages? I asked a number of women, "How important are your female friends?" Here are a few of the responses:

Carlie, a forty-one-year-old, married mother at home said: "Since I've become a full-time mother, my female friends have become very important in creating a new peer group, a sense of community and support as I tackle the difficult task of mothering."

Judy, a forty-three-year-old teacher, said: "I'm not married and haven't had a significant male relationship in five years. My female friends are therefore quite important. I confide in my friends. I've been able to share both strengths and weaknesses and receive love and acceptance."

Marie, a twenty-five-year-old, single, research analyst, said: "My three best friends provide emotional support and companionship. They also affirm me and help me with my struggles. I'm very close to my boyfriend, but my friends can relate to the fact that I'm a woman."

We need our friends as confidantes, as support players, as guides in rearing our children, as companions. They accept us, affirm us, and understand what it means to be a woman. They hold us accountable; they help us grow. When we're married, they provide an undergirding support for our marriages, and when we're single, they are the people we go to for in-depth understanding.

Usually our closest friends also share our spiritual journey. They share our values and pray for us in times of need. Said one woman, "If they have our true interests at heart, close friends will be willing to confront us when we're wrong, share our struggles, and encourage us with their hard-earned wisdom." While we can't choose our families, we can choose mates and close friends who will challenge us to grow closer to God. As they do this, our significant relationships are strengthened and deepened.

The stages of friendship

What is more, we need our friends our whole life long. According to Joel Block, our friendships with other women unfold over the life cycle, like a "friendship drama" with four acts.[17]

Act One begins around preadolescence when we are just beginning to struggle with puberty. We look for a girl to "passionately attach" ourselves to—a "first friend." These are tender relationships. "The events and contexts of childhood—embracing one another with tenderness, walking arm and arm, whispering confidences to one another, sleeping at each other's houses—are cherished memories to many women."[18]

Then comes Act Two: adolescence. Girlfriends become each other's constant companions. If they can't be together, they are attached via a telephone that seems to grow out of their heads. The soul mates talk about everything—that is, until they get mad at each other or pursue the same boy. But these friendships are less idyllic than earlier ones. Why? Guys are now on the scene, and girls compete like crazy for their attention. And if one girl "falls in love" with a boy, it's time for her friend to exit. Teenaged girls sometimes acknowledge that romantic relationships come before friendships. End of Act Two.

Act Three. While women continue to build friendships in their twenties, these years become "the least productive of close friendships." Block found in his research that women in their twenties had less desire for female companionship because women were often regarded "less as friends and more as diversions when a husband or lover was unavailable."[19] Men are the key players and women the second stringers during this decade. This pattern abates somewhat if women marry. Although their intimacy needs shift to marriage, they do seek out same-sex friends among neighbors or mothers of a child's playmates, or they reconnect with longtime friends.

Then comes Act Four: the "transitional thirties." Women turn back to female friendships in earnest in their early thirties. During this time, old friendships are renewed and become intimate again. New friends are eagerly sought. This ushers in the most productive years for female friendships which continue well into the fifties.[20]

While Block's "friendship drama" concludes when women hit their thirties, many women discover that their best female friendships occur as they approach their mid to late thirties and that these midlife friendships continue to ripen in their forties to fifties.

The reason? By the time women hit their mid thirties, they have settled into family life and/or career, and they have also "grown well into themselves." Identity issues have been resolved in the twenties, and some of those old competitive feelings have diminished. In their forties, but particularly in their fifties, women report that they are much more self-accepting than earlier in their lives. Said one forty-nine-year-old, "I no longer lust after my friend's beautiful house as I did in my thirties. I realize now that big, beautiful houses require a lot of work, time, and money just to keep up. And I have much better things to do with my life than care for property."

There are other reasons that friendships can blossom in midlife. Not only do we become less competitive and more accepting, but our children begin to leave the nest in earnest. No longer are we racing to soccer and baseball practices every evening and most weekends, so we now have more time for friendships. And we need those midlife friends who will allow us to mourn the empty nest, who will encourage us in our work, who will be there just to attend a movie or share a meal.

Mostly, in midlife we need our menopausal buddies who, like us, are experiencing the hormonal crazies, the erratic rising and falling of hormones that some of us experience in our forties and early fifties. Said an executive of an international organization, "This fall my husband and I confront the empty nest, and we will miss our children greatly. Add that to the fact that at forty-seven I am premenopausal, and you'll understand why I need my friends as never before."

During my forties when I was premenopausal and suffering from mood swings due to erratic estrogen levels (I felt as if I had constant PMS), I desperately needed a close female friend. I had just moved from Sparta, New Jersey, to Washington, D.C., a city about which President Harry Truman purportedly said, "If you want a friend in Washington, get a dog."

Well, I didn't have a dog, and I didn't have any friends. What I did have were two adolescent daughters wrapped up in their own lives and a husband who worked long hours at a new and demanding job. At that time I was not a psychologist but a writer and a mother at home, struggling to figure out what to do with the next stage of my life. My children needed me less (or thought they did), and I was tired of writing books.

While I was struggling with myself and my family, I went to a women's group at church one Wednesday and found a pair of compassionate brown eyes staring at me. This woman and I started to talk. In time Eleanor and I began to meet at a local cafe, and soon we were sharing our problems, our struggles, our secrets. For a while we met with another woman weekly for breakfast, creating an informal menopausal support group. We didn't call it that, of course. (The other two wouldn't allow me to, so I called us "women of a certain age.")

During that year Eleanor and I helped Connie face the death of her husband, and among the three of us we sent several kids to college. We laughed together and cried on occasion. Sometimes we crawled into Connie's old station wagon to pray. Out of those early morning conversations Eleanor and I decided we wanted to do something for young mothers, and in 1987 Home by Choice, Inc., a national support group for mothers, was born. For the past twelve years, even with very busy lives, we have been close friends. We get together about once a week, just to talk and laugh together. My friendship with Eleanor has been one of the richest of my entire life, and I tell her jokingly that she has been inducted into my Friendship Hall of Fame, to which she responds with good-natured laughter.

We need other women across the years—as preteens, as thirtysomethings, and as women of a certain age. We also need each other in the winter of our lives when spouses may have died and children have long grown and gone. Our friendships with other women are, as Shere Hite found when she interviewed several thousand women, "some of the happiest, most fulfilling" personal relationships of our lives.[21]

9

• • •

Key Players and Second Stringers

In addition to helping us grow and giving us

pleasure and providing aid and comfort,

our intimate friendships shelter us from loneliness.

Judith Viorst, *Necessary Losses*

One day eight-year-old Tricia came up to her mother and said with exasperation, "Mom, I don't have anyone to play with." After questioning her somewhat shy daughter, Heather learned that Tricia's best friend, Pam, was going shopping with her mother and that her next best friend, Janice, had a soccer game that morning. So she explained to Tricia one of the things she had learned about friends: we need key players and second stringers in our playing field at all times to have a sufficient team of friends.

"What's a key player?" asked Tricia, curling up in her mother's lap.

"She's one of your closest friends. Sometimes you have only one, although most people have two or three at any given time. But you also have a number of other friends who share one of your special interests. These are second stringers. You have friends to play dolls with. Or another friend to go camping with. Or another friend who loves to play board games. They are not less important friends. We just spend less time with them."

What Heather was trying to teach her daughter was that we have different levels of friendship in life. No one friend can supply all we need. Just as a husband cannot share all our interests or meet all our emotional needs, no one female friend can be all things to us.

Nor are all friendships the same. George Santayana said, "Friendship is almost always the union of a part of one mind with a part of another; people are friends in spots." And if we limit ourselves to one or two friends, we may miss the richness that a variety of friends can offer.

Key players coach us through tough times

First of all, who are the key players in our Friendship Hall of Fame?

A key player has seen us through some of life's tough experiences, the emotionally intense times. She has consoled us when we've lost a job or a boyfriend. Perhaps she has walked us through a divorce or even the death of a family member. She has comforted us when we felt little comfort existed.

This past Christmas Day Kristie called to tell me that Sherry's baby had been delivered, dead, at term. Her voice cracked with emotion. "Sherry knew the baby was dead only hours before delivery. When the doctor said he sensed no heartbeat, at first Sherry didn't get it. Then the truth sank in."

In addition to emotional support, Kristie gave Sherry and her family practical help and her presence. Kristie called family and friends and attended the funeral where Sherry and Mark gave speeches to all assembled, sharing their hopes and dreams for their baby, Catherine Joan. At the funeral, Kristie watched as Sherry and Mark leaned into each other when their voices broke and they could barely speak. "I'm grateful Sherry and I have a close friendship," says Kristie, "because now when she needs me I can be there for her."

Key players know our secrets

Our key players know our anguish when our teenagers mess up their lives. They listen as we tell them about how our family or boyfriends or husbands have hurt us. Gracie and Alexis were in grad school working on their doctorates when Gracie's marriage collapsed. And Alexis was there to listen and encourage. Now as Alexis struggles with her teenagers, she calls Gracie almost daily. Now Gracie is the one who listens and provides emotional support. "How could I not be there for Alexis after all she has done for me?" she asks.

Key players keep secrets

We trust key players not to betray us. Lisa, at twenty-seven, says she tells her best friend Eve things she would never tell anyone else except her husband. She trusts her "absolutely" and "knows she'd never tell what I confide in her. She really sees me and knows who I am. We connect at a very deep level, which is a first for me."

"Over the years," says Jackie, twenty-two, "I've had friends tell me about venereal disease, infertility, money troubles, depression, suicidal thoughts, sexual abuse, sexual experiences, affairs, drug use, abortion, and incest. I've heard everything! I'm honored that people entrust their secrets with me because I know how difficult it is to do. Some people have so much pain in their lives that I think they have to share it with someone. Maybe they think I'm empathetic, but they definitely think I can keep a secret."

Key players are not judgmental

Our key players have been there for us when we needed them. Entrusted with our darkest secrets and most vulnerable hurts, they are open, accepting, and nonjudgmental. How else could we show them our hearts? Sandra, a fifty-year-old second grade teacher, describes her best friend, Lee: "With her I am honest about my innermost feelings, fears, thoughts, and ideas. Lee has proven to be accepting, kind, and honest with me about herself. She is willing to tell me what she thinks if I ask, but she doesn't expect me to take her advice. She allows me to be me."

This doesn't mean, of course, that our closer friends won't confront us when needed. In healthy, close relationships there is always a degree of accountability.

Key players inconvenience themselves for us

Key players will come to us in the middle of the night if we need them. They hear the pain in our voices when we've had a major disappointment and don't have to be persuaded to come to our rescue. Sometimes they will do for us what our extended family can't do because of physical distance. Even Proverbs 27:10 says, "Do not forsake your friend and the friend of your father, and do not go to your brother's house when disaster strikes you—better a neighbor nearby than a brother far away."

I remember the day I learned Eleanor was a twenty-four hour friend. She told me she had been up since three in the morning in response to a phone call. She had left her comfortable suburban home to drive to a drug-infested area of Washington to pick up Karen, a woman she had worked with while the director of Bethany Women's Shelter. As I listened to my friend speak of helping Karen find a place to stay in the middle of the night (Karen had been booted out of her apartment by a boyfriend), I told her, "Ells, this really comforts me. Now I know that I can count on you if I ever have a middle-of-the-night emergency." We laughed, but I know she'd come if I needed her.

In this chancy world, it is no small comfort to have, in addition to a key player husband, one or two friends we can count on during life's inevitable crises. Some people don't have anyone to come when they call, so we are blessed indeed if we can, on occasion, presume on a friendship.

Key players are forever friends

No matter where we live and how many oceans separate us or how many years have passed, some key players remain central figures in our lives. After returning from a New Year's vacation, I checked my phone messages and heard one from my friend Ros. The sound of her voice reminds me of our friendship, begun twenty-two years ago when I moved to London. Ros, a therapist and prime mover in London L'Abri, a church-house ministry, welcomed us, and we became fast friends.

When Ros and her eleven-year-old daughter, Sarah, were here last summer, we sat on my screened-in porch in the August heat and humidity, reminiscing. Ros reminded me that on one of our mini-vacations together some twenty-two years earlier, three-year-old Kris had taken gum out of her mouth and offered it to Ros. Ros immediately popped it into her own mouth. "Now, that's true friendship," she said, smiling. And so it is.

Once a bond is forged in the fire of intense emotional experience and it endures, these women may become our forever friends, whether we see them frequently or seldom. If they live far away, we pick up where we left off when we next see them. We have the ability to suspend dialogue, but not our feelings, which remain constant despite the distance and the years that may separate us.

In *Necessary Losses* Judith Viorst calls these "crossroads friends." These are friends who are important for "what was." In these friendships we shared a crucial, now past, time of life—"a time, perhaps when we roomed in college together; served a stint in the U.S. Air Force together; or worked as eager young singles in Manhattan together; or went through pregnancy, birth and those first difficult years of motherhood together."[1] Viorst says we have a special, tender intimacy with these crossroads friends that is dormant, waiting to be revived periodically.[2]

Cynthia lives in Ohio and her friend Lucy, in Maryland, Yet she describes their friendship as "almost telepathic," transcending time and distance. "We hardly ever see each other," says Cynthia, "but we know that when we need each other, we're right there—no matter what."

"My best friend Maxine lives in Thailand," says Holly, "but whenever I think of her it's almost as if she's here. This past Christmas she came back for a visit, and I drove to a friend's house to pick her up. When she opened the door, it was almost like the time since our last visit instantly compressed. I felt no awkwardness, no distance.

"Maxine is the friend I always dreamed about. Yet if you look at our lives, you might ask 'Why are they friends?' From the outside, we look completely different. We are different nationalities, different races, and we live on completely opposite sides of the world.

"But we are so similar. We have tempestuous emotions at times and can be extremely flaky. Our friends were always teasing us because we were forever driving our cars into garage posts. She was my flamboyant sidekick; both of us favored bright, dramatic clothes. We spent tons of time together when she was posted in D.C. We went to the beach, plays, the ballet. The day she left the U.S. was one of the saddest of my life. Luckily, we've kept in touch. I've been to England and she's been back here. Phone calls are expensive—fifty to eighty dollars—so we don't make them often, but we've been known to do it in times of crisis.

"When I broke up with Lowell, I called her at seven in the morning on a Saturday! Poor Max! She never gets up before noon on Saturday, but she listened and was loving and encouraging. Max is the greatest. A completely admirable person. She is very independent—I could never move alone to a new country. She also has the greatest faith in God. I really look up to her. Through a prison ministry she works with drug dealers who are in jail for life. Most importantly, though, she is my friend for life. I know how her mind works and vice versa. I can count on her."

So our key players may live in London, Ohio, or Bangkok. Or they may live next door. What counts is their dependability, acceptance, trustworthiness, love, and longevity.

Second stringers

If we could fill our lives with key players, why would we even be interested in second stringers?

Key players are few and far between. These are our closest friends—our soul mates—and they may not all be local or even available to us as often as we like. Besides, it's important to spread friendship needs around so our lives will be richer. Second stringers enable us to do this. These are the people with whom we share common interests and goals.

Second stringers can be divided into "A list" and "B list" people. "A list" women are those who could possibly become best friends. While these women share similar interests and values, they simply haven't been around long enough or gone through enough intense emotional experiences with us to develop into close friends. These friendships await testing.

Then there are those on the "B list" who are occasional friends. With these friends we share common interests rather than confidences. Judith Viorst calls these "special interest friends" who share sports, work projects, causes. "The emphasis in these friendships is on doing rather than being."[3] We are not necessarily committed to these relationships and may never be. Months can go by without seeing our occasional friends, and neither party feels guilty. Yet when our lives do intersect at times, we are the richer for it.

"Renee is possibly the most private person I know," says Megan. "She doesn't seem to mind if we don't see each other for a month or two, and she tells me I see her more than most! Yet she adds a lot to my life even in these small increments; she's incredibly sophisticated, funny, and really self-reliant. She's one the few people I can do high-brow things with. We go to artsy movies, hang out at coffee bars, discuss plays. I'm not as close to Renee as I am Alicia, my best friend, but Alicia loves country music and political science—things I hate!"

Sarah's husband, a psychology professor, dislikes opera, so Sarah purchases season tickets to the Kennedy Center with her friend Rita. They are opera buffs together, but not bosom pals.

While key players nourish our deepest selves and these are the women we tend to see most frequently, we need to have enough "A" and "B list" women in our lives to provide balance and to meet a larger range of interests. I didn't always believe this. In my early forties I would have told you I was an introvert who needed only a few close friends or soul mates. I was focused on acquiring those few key players and didn't consciously value second stringers.

However, in my thirties when I was attempting to publish my second book and failing to find an interested publisher (nine turned me down), I started a writers group in the tiny town of Sparta, New Jersey. Each week three of us met for lunch to share ideas and encourage each other. These women helped me persevere until I finally found a publisher. One of the other two women has since published eighty articles in newspapers and magazines—and has become a treasured friend. This was my first adult induction into a special interest group that worked.

Finally, a new category

In addition to key players and second stringers, I would also add another category I call "serendipitous friends." *Webster's* defines *serendipity* as "the faculty of finding valuable or agreeable things not sought for." So serendipitous friends are those women who enter our lives though we do not choose them. Perhaps we aren't particularly attracted to them at first or they don't appear similar to us in important ways.

One woman remembers a neighbor whose superficiality drove her into a frenzy. She was ready to pull the plug on this relationship one day when Joan came over for dinner. "God," she prayed, "I've had it with Joan. I can't talk to her about anything meaningful." As she returned from the kitchen, casserole in hand, Joan looked up at her and said, "My husband had an affair during our last military posting." This woman eased herself into a chair, and they were off and running on what became a rich and rewarding friendship.

So serendipitous friends enter our lives and surprise us and enlarge us by their presence. And we are glad they came.

"Janet and I could not be more different," says Judy, a speech writer in her twenties. "She is super-rational, I'm an emotional yo-yo. She reads books on the Middle East for fun, I barely ever pick up a paper. When we go out, we almost always go to a restaurant because at least we both love to eat! Janet has been really good for me, though," says Judy. "Although we sort of fell into the friendship, we've learned a lot. I'm helping her to be more emotive, she gives me a rational spin on crises. Plus, I take lessons on how to be a friend from her. Everybody loves her—she's been a bridesmaid in twelve weddings."

What about "chance friendships"?

As a consequence of several serendipitous friendships that seemingly defy logic, I've learned to look beyond those things that sociologists say draw us together: similarity of social class, education, lifestyle. While these factors operate in most of our friendships, they shouldn't be used to exclude people who might enrich our lives.

Besides, there's an overarching principle that guides our deepest friendships. We do not always choose our friends, says C. S. Lewis: "In reality, a few years difference in the dates of our birth, a few more miles between certain houses, the choice of one university instead of another, posting to different regiments, the accident of a topic being raised at a first meeting—any of these chances might have kept us apart. But, for a Christian, there are, strictly speaking, no chances. A secret master of ceremonies has been at work."[4]

While we may think we choose the key players and even the second stringers in our lives, Lewis says that in reality God chooses us to befriend each other. If you reflect back on your own life and examine important friendships, you will probably see you needed each one to teach you something terribly important about yourself or life. And you will notice that each of these friends came along at just the right time to teach you patiently and lovingly what you needed to learn.

Rennie, who had a desperate relationship with her mother, believes that Sally's friendship during her teens not only saved her sanity but enabled her to be the friend she is today to many women. Sally's friendship provided a way for Rennie to escape her chaotic home for hours on end. From Sally, another female, Rennie learned she could be close to her own sex. Today Rennie is said to be everybody's closest friend.

Who sends these necessary and treasured friends? Who indeed.

10

· · ·

The Art of Friendship

But if you tame me, it will be as if the sun came to shine on my life.
Antoine de Saint-Exupéry

S ometimes I am accosted by a man or woman at a party who wants to discuss the writing life. Usually this person assumes the ability to write is a gift bestowed by the gods. "All I need to do," he or she thinks, "is sit in front of my computer and wait for inspiration, like lightning, to strike. Mesmerized, I then type an unending flow of words which never need revision."

Somewhat amused, I feel compelled to set the record straight. "Mine is not a major talent or gift," I say, "and if I had waited for inspiration, I would still not be published. Writing is hard work, and I revise everything at least three times."

At this point in the conversation, the inquirer is no longer enamored of the writing life and usually changes the subject. We talk until one of us moves on. Then I remember the words of novelist Vladimir Nabokov: "I have written—often several times—every word I have ever published. My pencils outlast their erasers."

As for inspiration, novelist Frank Yerby said, "I quit writing if I feel inspired, because I know I'm going to have to throw it away. Writing a novel is like building a wall, brick by brick; only amateurs believe in inspiration."

Just as writing is an art that requires work and perseverance, so the art of friendship requires thoughtfulness and effort. Just as writers work at the craft of writing, so those who are rich in friends work in crafting friendships. And we become experts, in some measure, through the acquisition of social skills and the observance of friendship rituals. In fact, *Webster's* defines an art as a "skill acquired by experience, study or observation, such as the art of making friends."

Most of us would agree it is simply not enough to sit at home in the evening, watching television while we wait for potential friends to beat a path to our door. Extroverts know this and surround themselves with people. Introverts seek out a few deep friendships. And those who are shy or who have been rejected? While they may find it hard, they must have faith that they can make good friends in time and have the courage to reach out.

Psychologist Harville Hendrix recounts a conversation with a client that illustrates this point.

"Harville," he said to me as he slumped into the chair, "I feel really terrible. I just don't have any friends."

I was sympathetic with him. "You must be very sad. It's lonely not having any friends."

"Yeah. I can't seem to…I don't know. There are no friends in my life. I keep looking and looking, and I can't seem to find any."

Walter was locked into a view of the world that went something like this: wandering around the world were people on whose forehead were stamped the words "Friends of Walter," and his job was merely to search until he found them.

"Walter," I said with a sigh, "do you understand why you don't have any friends?"

He perked up. "No. Tell me!"

"The reason you don't have any friends is that there aren't any friends out there."

His shoulders slumped.

I was relentless. "That's right," I told him. "There are no friends out there. What you want does not exist." I let him stew in this sad state of affairs for a few seconds. Then I leaned forward in my chair and said, "Walter—listen to me! All people in the world are strangers. If you want a friend, you're going to have to go out and make one!"[1]

Hendrix is right. Turning strangers into friends is what friendship is all about—for all of us. And how do we turn those strangers into friends?

First we have to meet them

A single, thirty-year-old computer programmer in Seattle says she works six days a week. Not surprisingly, she has little social life and few close friends. Fortunately, she's beginning to understand that creating a rich social life will require changes in her lifestyle.

We need to pursue our own interests. We will be happier and more fulfilled if we are chasing our dreams and snaring them rather than waiting for someone to come along and validate our worthiness. Classes, seminars, and clubs exist so that like-minded souls can come together over their personal passions, whether it is skiing, biking, hiking, running, photography, great literature, history, travel, or cooking. From scuba diving to wreath shaping, chances are our interests are covered. We can network through the groups attached to our jobs, local universities and museums, even bookstores or athletic shops.

We also need to deepen our spiritual life. Churches are not only places to worship but places where we can meet others who will help us grow spiritually and personally. Singles ministries, Bible studies, missions classes, visiting the elderly, and tutoring the learning-disadvantaged will enlarge our perspective and give us people of different ages to relate to. It will also make us more compassionate and grateful to be alive.

Then, we can analyze the people already in our lives. Are there potential friendships just waiting to be developed? It's a whole lot easier to deepen friendships then to start from scratch. We can ask coworkers to lunch and acquaintances to share various activities. Sometimes friendships just await developing.

If we are married and employed, we can consciously set aside time for developing friendships with other women, perhaps devoting one lunch hour or one evening per week to spend with same-sex friends. Husbands need time with their buddies just as we need to talk to our female friends. We will have more to contribute to our marriage if each of us has some outside interests and same-sex friendships.

Having couple friends over for dinner at least once a month not only enriches our marriages but provides intellectual stimulation. Remember, we're building friendships for those midlife years when the kids are gone and friendships will become more important than ever.

If we're married and mothers at home, we can have other mothers and their children in for coffee, lunch, or tea weekly. This is a great way for children to enhance their social skills as we meet our own needs for time with other women. We can even start a neighborhood moms' support group to meet weekly or biweekly and hire a baby-sitter for the kids so they can play out of earshot at the other end of the house—or at another house. Time permitting, we can find a passion and volunteer. Groups like Mothers First, Moms' Clubs, MOPS, and Mothers at Home are meeting places for bright, articulate, like-minded moms. Heidi Brennan says, "I get all my friendship needs met by volunteering at Mothers at Home."

Hone communication skills

To have close friends, we must be able to share our deepest selves. This means we speak openly and honestly about who we are—our interests, values, personal history, and feelings. We share our strengths and our weaknesses as well.

This is not to say we tell everybody every terrible thing that has ever happened to us. Only needy people spill secrets indiscriminately. One woman blurted out to strangers that she had a miserable marriage and, she added, "So do most women I know." Sadly, she drove others away even though she desperately needed help. But she needed to talk to a confidante or a professional about her marriage rather than expect sympathy or understanding from a group of strangers.

What's important is to share enough of ourselves to be authentic. In friendships, we usually start with shared interests and values and then move on to problem areas as trust in the friendship develops. The key is timing. We need to share appropriately and give the relationship time to grow and deepen.

Learn to listen deeply

Kristie, a thirty-nine-year-old mother at home, has developed her listening skills through the Stephens ministry at her church. She not only practices these skills on her husband and two children, Meggie and Matt, she also is a good listener for her close friends. "I pay attention to body language—eye contact, folded arms, leaning forward or into the chair," says Kristie, "and I try to hear the unspoken message underneath the words." Obviously, this requires sensitivity to the person in front of us—her facial expression, body movements, tone of voice. A colleague at the mental health center where I work says we get 90 percent of our information from the nonverbal cues that we assimilate and interpret and only 10 percent from actual words.

Part of listening deeply is learning to communicate warmth and empathy to our friends. Jerry Authier, in writing about good communication, says that warmth has three major dimensions.[2] First, we communicate our willingness to listen. Then we show respect for our friend's worth, integrity, and abilities. And finally, we help our friend to tell her story. How? Through good eye contact, clarifying what she has said, and asking questions. What kinds of questions lead to deeper communication? Authier suggests that we ask open-ended questions (How satisfied are you with your relationships?) rather than closed questions (Are you satisfied with your relationships?).

In showing empathy, Authier suggests sitting closer to our friend, leaning forward, and focusing on the friend's feelings rather than the facts or events.[3] The message we send is that we're really concerned about our friend's welfare, not just events or information traded.

If we listen well, our friends will feel understood, comforted, enlarged in their deepest selves. However, we need to make sure that we do not listen most or all of the time. In my friendships, I make sure I get approximately 50 percent of the airtime. At some point I learned that reciprocity is central. That means I don't take up all the airtime, nor do I allow friends to do it either. Some of us have trained our friends to be selfish by our doing all the listening. But if we're honest, we must admit that at times when we leave our friends, we are a little blue or lonely, feeling as if our friends don't care enough about us to ask key questions.

A young woman said recently that her three closest friends are lost in their own lives. One has lost her job, and the other two are immersed in serious love relationships. "They never ask me any questions. Sure, they have reasons to be focused on themselves, but don't my needs count too?" Obviously, a friend in crisis mode will demand more airtime, but how much is enough? Even when we are in crisis, we need to be conscious and sensitive to the needs of others.

When a friend is in trouble, she doesn't want you to solve her problem. Rather she needs a compassionate listener. If she asks for advice, give it. But don't try to "fix" her problems. If practical help is appropriate—meals, baby-sitting—extend that, so your friend will know you care. But it's unhealthy to become a rescuer in a relationship and take charge of your friend's finances, children, or marital problems.

Ask good questions

We need to avoid superficiality except when warming up or ending a conversation. Ask your friend how she is *really* and listen carefully. You can begin with "What's going on in your life?" Most of the time people will give you an entrée that you can parlay into a deep conversation. Seize those opportunities.

Marla says, "I encourage friends to tell me their stories by just asking some simple questions and then listening. I usually begin with something innocuous, and as my friend begins to talk, I take mental notes.

Each successive question builds on some key idea she has just expressed. I view listening and asking questions as pulling a thread out of a ball of yarn. Each question builds on what I've heard or intuited, and as I pull or probe, the skein unravels. My friend—or even a stranger—will tell me her deepest struggles."

Is Marla being manipulative or nosy? She doesn't think so. She understands that some people are more private than others, but she finds that most want to be heard and understood.

Recently when Marla went to purchase glasses, she asked the sales clerk to help her find a pair so she wouldn't be invisible. "Midlife women can become invisible, you know," she said laughing. Then Marla asked this woman in her forties if she found midlife changes hard. How did she handle body image changes? They moved from her concern about her wrinkles to the flooding of her home to her fear that she might have breast cancer (she was scheduled for a mammogram the next week) to her hunger for deeper spirituality—all in forty-five minutes. At the same time they selected the glasses and joked about midlife women with their elevated testosterone levels and greater aggressiveness. When Marla left, she felt lifted by their laughter and conversation and planned to stop by the next week to see how the woman's mammogram turned out.

At times, learning to ask good questions can lead to much weightier matters. I shall long remember the day I met Judy. She was about sixty pounds overweight with bleached blond hair. Wrapped in a faded navy sweatshirt, she sat alone at the only semi-vacant table in the whole Georgetown University cafeteria. I slid my tray onto the table and sat down. "Are you a student at Georgetown?" I asked, knowing that the university had a number of middle-aged women returning to finish degrees.

"No, " she said, "I'm a patient in the Oncology Department." Taking a deep breath as if she were about to jump off the high diving board, she said, "I have metastasized breast cancer."

For a second, I was speechless. "Just what does that mean?"

"I have a tumor on the wall on my bladder and I've had a nephrotomy." Judy said that she had discovered she had breast cancer in 1989, that she and her husband were out of money, and that she was now filing for Social

Security. In addition, she depended on the kindnesses of her Georgetown physicians who continued to treat her even though they might never be paid.

I asked her if she had a support group of other cancer patients or good friends to talk to.

"I went to a support group but found that I have a compulsive need to take care of everybody, so I never went back. My friends have withdrawn. This illness is more than they can handle. And my twenty-three-year-old daughter is about to fall apart." Judy choked up but fought back the tears.

"Do you believe in angels?" she asked suddenly. Then without waiting for an answer, she said she felt angels were protecting her as she struggled with her disease. "I want to write a book about my experience with cancer because so many women are afraid of breast cancer."

I gave her the names of several publishers who were gathering for a convention at a local hotel the following weekend. "Oh, that's where I used to work," Judy said. She spoke of the disparity between her former responsible, wage-earning life and her current poverty. I sympathized with her and encouraged her to find meaning and purpose through writing even at this terrible time in her life. Her face brightened as I talked about writing and publishing. "I want to leave something behind, a legacy," she said. "Maybe it will help my daughter who's denying my illness.

"Sometimes I just want to go away and be quiet and enjoy whatever time I have left. Other times I want to fight for my life. I want to start a support group for other women with cancer—one that emphasizes life rather than death."

After two hours we rose to leave the cafeteria. I gave Judy my name and phone number, as well as the names of several groups where she might find support. We stood, hesitant to part, two women facing vastly different struggles. I walked back to the library to continue working on this book. And Judy rose to continue facing the immense challenge she has bravely confronted for eight years.

"You're a brave woman," I told her. A woman who can confront her own death and still get excited about the possibility of starting a support group or writing a book has a resilient spirit.

We took each other's hands as we said good-bye. Then Judy cocked her head and asked, "Are you an angel?"

I laughed. "No, I'm definitely *not* an angel. But it's no coincidence that you and I met today." As an afterthought I added, "Maybe your guardian angel saw to that."

We parted and I returned to the library, feeling that I had just experienced a rare gift. I had met a woman, a stranger, and for two hours we had talked of life and death, her family, my profession, God, and angels. She said that although her Irish husband cheered her up he was struggling to handle her illness. Whatever he gave her, I sensed she needed more. She needed to talk to another woman, someone who could also speak the language of feelings and the heart.

Practice unsolicited acts of kindness

"Practice random acts of kindness and senseless acts of beauty" is an adage for the nineties. Friendship between women thrives when it contains nurturing, even maternal acts. We especially enjoy small or unexpected gifts that meet an unexpressed need. My friend Ree, a wonderful cook, has on several occasions left dinner in a brown paper bag on my doorstep when she has known I've had a numbingly busy day. Imagine my joy when I've come home in the evening, tired and hungry, to find a complete meal and dessert wrapped in foil.

Birthday parties are special times for the expression of friendship. We can throw a surprise dinner party for the birthday person or appear at her house for breakfast on the actual day, oversized muffins and designer coffee in hand. If we're moms at home, we can plan a luncheon or have friends in for tea. One of my friends who works part-time invited seven women for lunch on my fifty-third birthday which happily coincided with her day off. On her fortieth, several of us surprised her with a celebration she feared would not take place since her husband was out of the country on business.

Even in "unbirthday" times we can make each other feel special. Allison writes notes, calls her friends frequently, and when they come over, she buys flowers and makes special name cards for their plates. In the dead of winter, we can remember our friends with a bunch of violets or a book. When

I was a divorced mother in London, my friend Ros would sometimes show up unexpectedly on my doorstep in the early evening with a "sweet" in hand. My girls would be in bed, and we would sit in the living room, two single women, sharing from our hearts while laughing over a dessert and a pot of English tea.

Be conscious of reciprocity

We must not make our friends do all the work of friendship. Friendship is a two-way street. If one insists on being nurtured and the other is always the nurturer, a codependent, unequal relationship evolves, and the nurturer is bound to feel resentful and exploited.

Of course, we can nurture in different ways. While providing physical acts of nurture may come easily to one woman—bringing a meal, running an errand—another may be better schooled in providing psychological nurture—listening, talking through a problem. The key is that both feel they give something to the relationship; one is not always a taker while the other is a giver. Even if a friend is younger and less experienced, it's important to view her as an equal who has as much to offer as you have. Beware of unequal friendships. These relationships say as much about the giver as the taker.

It is important for the health of the relationship that we do our share of the calling, the gift giving, the listening. Jill, a new wife, noticed that her husband made most of the calls to his friends and that when he was with them he spent far too much time listening to them talk about their lives. She asked her husband, Peter, how this made him feel. He admitted that it diminished his self-esteem, so they tried an experiment. Peter stopped calling these friends regularly, and several never contacted him again. While it was painful for him to face the truth about these relationships, he became more cognizant of making deeper friendships and allowing others to help carry the responsibility for the relationship. Now he has richer, deeper, more equal friendships with other men.

As a rule of thumb, we need to take a hard look at relationships where one party does all the work. This signifies a lack of interest or capacity for reciprocity on the other person's part, and is that really a friendship?

Keep commitments

None of us likes fair-weather friends who flee just as we're heading into a crisis. How many women with breast cancer have discovered that their friends cannot handle their disease? How many women whose husbands are leaving have friends walk away at the same time? It's not always possible or comfortable to mix couples and singles, but it's good for both on occasion. All come away with an enlarged perspective. Don and I have single friends who've greatly enriched our lives. Karen and Linda paid Don a high compliment when they said he was "just one of us." When I was a single mother, I needed to be with couples. After all, we were all *families* together. It's important to be a comforting presence in hard times, because our time will likely come.

Of course, friendship is sometimes inconvenient. The price is high in terms of time and emotional energy, but that's part of any close friendship. Friendships may necessitate sacrifice, which means we can't be deeply committed to many friends at once. We only have so much time and emotional energy, and many of us have prior commitments to our husband and children. But when our friends are truly in need, we need to be accessible.

Be comfortable in your own skin

Finally, a key component in the art of friendship is less a skill than a state of being. To be most effective at friendship we need first to make friends with ourselves. In *Necessary Losses* Judith Viorst says we have to have a self to be a friend.[4] What does it mean to have a self? It means we have an inner core. We like ourselves for the most part, and we can be alone and enjoy our own company. We don't use our friends as a way of escaping our feelings of boredom, emptiness, or even self-hatred. We need to be comfortable inside our own skin to be comfortable in friendships. We need to develop our own interests, hobbies, and goals that we occasionally pursue alone. We need to balance time spent with our friends with time spent in solitude.

Solitude restores our souls. It is in solitude, as well as in the company of others, that we come to know who we really are. And if we must confront some emptiness and pain, so be it. This must be faced and worked through, or we will run from aloneness all our lives. To be a good friend, we have to occasionally fly solo.

Recently, Maxine, my daughter Holly's good friend, came for a visit from Bangkok. A child of divorce, she has finally come to terms with her feelings of loneliness. Maxine works for the British Embassy, and after living in Washington, D.C. for three years, she has been sent to Thailand. Once there, she prayed and prayed, asking God to send her a best friend. Finally He spoke to her: "Who am I?"

"At first I ignored Him," said Maxine, "but finally I saw it. That's what He is—my friend. Since then I've felt I'm never alone. And when I feel lonely—and I do at times—I know the feelings will pass. I used to fear they would destroy me."

Each of us must learn to deal with our loneliness in order to be a close friend to another. Otherwise we will choke the life out of our closest friendships by clinging and demanding too much and then be angry when our friends refuse to meet our expectations. Those who failed to receive adequate parental love and nurture in childhood need to recognize that they will be prone to greater loneliness as adults than people whose needs were adequately met.

But all of us can find, as Maxine did, that God can become the closest friend we have ever known. When He is with us, we are never bereft or completely alone.

Keep practicing

Just as we sink years into honing musical, artistic, and literary talents, we have to practice being good friends to those who enter our lives. We learn to erase wrong words and eradicate injuries through forgiveness. We learn to become emotionally accessible to close friends even at inconvenient times. We spend time together, sharing, listening, giving kindnesses, and providing emotional support. In the process, we learn to be patient with ourselves and others. In the end, we see that friendship is the fire we warm ourselves by in the sometimes lonely, often tumultuous journey called life.

One of my favorite books is *The Little Prince* by Antoine de Saint-Exupéry. This lovely children's book has a deep commentary on the nature of friendship. Perhaps you have read this to your children. If so, you may recall the passage when the fox asks the Little Prince to "tame" him. The fox tells the Little Prince that once tamed, he will listen for the sound of the Little Prince's footstep; it will be "like music" calling him out of his burrow. And when the fox sees wheat fields, the color of the wheat will remind him of the Little Prince's hair and he "shall love to listen to the wind in the wheat." With great profundity, the fox says that "one only understands the things one tames.... If you want a friend, tame me."

So patiently the Little Prince tames the fox. They establish friendship rituals. The Little Prince comes to see the fox at the same time each day. And when the Little Prince must depart and return to his planet, the fox cries. The Little Prince, somewhat obtusely, suggests the grief is all the fox's fault, but the fox teaches him a great truth. "It is only with the heart that one can see rightly; what is essential is invisible to the eye." And then he adds that it is the time we "waste" on our friends that makes them unique and important.

Such wise words. It is the time we spend with our friends, it is the "taming" of the heart and the rituals in the art of friendship that make us unique in all the world to each other.

It is just as the fox, who understood friendship, said.

11

• • •

Surviving Conflict in Friendships

I've never lost a friendship through a disagreement or fight.

Mae Jones, age ninety

S hannon waited impatiently at a local deli. Her friend April was twenty minutes late. A stickler for punctuality (especially on her time), Shannon fumed that she had left work punctually to cool her heels, wasting time.

When April finally arrived, she avoided eye contact with Shannon and neglected to apologize. Instead she said, "I had a hard time leaving the office."

"We could have rescheduled if you were too busy," Shannon replied.

"No, no, we've already rescheduled once."

After the two women were seated in the back of the restaurant, they spoke of the upcoming holidays, their families, their jobs. They stayed on a safe, superficial plane. As they talked, Shannon felt a chill settle around their table.

Earlier there had been a breach in their friendship. The last time they were together April had shared intense, personal feelings about a painful relationship. Instead of just listening to her feelings, Shannon had tried to "fix" the problem. Later April called, coldly angry. "I wanted you to be my friend, not my therapist," she said. Shannon smarted at her words but apologized, admitting she had come on too strong.

Shannon had thought they had patched up their differences, but today she wasn't so sure. April was cool, and after only thirty minutes she looked at her watch. "Gotta go," she said abruptly. Shannon had just ordered her coffee, but as April walked away, she rose, leaving it untouched.

Their friendship, like the coffee, has cooled. Will it revive itself? Will these two women deal with the negative feelings they both have? What's Shannon's responsibility to herself and to April at this point? Shannon doesn't know. We only have emotional energy for a few in-depth relationships. If this had happened in a relationship with a best friend, Shannon would have gone home, called her up, and said, "What was going on today?" But April is a new friend, and she may not exert herself.

Some suggestions to handle conflict

This episode raises an intriguing question: how do we handle conflict in our relationships? Some women avoid conflict in their deepest relationships (although they may talk to their mothers and sisters about their true feelings), while others tell their friends whenever they are angry. Which is the right approach?

According to a 1990 Gallup Mirror of America survey, most Americans avoid clashes with their friends. When asked, "Do you ever get into serious arguments with your friends?" only 13 percent said yes. Eighty percent gave a resounding no, indicating that they failed to challenge the relationship by discussing negative feelings.

Can the majority of Americans be wrong? Is it best to stuff our negative feelings and avoid threatening the friendship? Or should we speak the truth as we perceive it? We know that sooner or later in any relationship negative feelings will surface. But apparently most women don't talk honestly about their feelings or confront a friend when a misunderstanding occurs.

Writer Sherryl Kleinman says that while women are the intimacy experts, many "end their relationships without warning or 'drift away.'"[1] Why can't women use their considerable social skills to solve problems and friendships? Kleinman believes we want "peaceable relationships" that we can idealize. Yet it is a fallacy to think of friendship as such a "pure" relationship that it can't be worked on.

So what happens when a friendship is in trouble? We stuff our negative feelings and paint on a fake, tense smile. We either make elaborate excuses about why we can't spend time together, or we simply dance away. Kleinman writes, "Ironically, the voluntary nature of friendship—the very thing that makes it special—also makes it easier for partners to exit."

I have danced away from relationships and, I imagine, so have you. Even if we don't pull away physically, we may absent ourselves emotionally. Tasha, who grew up in a family with a lot of conflict, fears anger. So she handles conflict in close friendships by being emotionally absent. "When I'm angry at a close friend, I'm there, but not there," she says. "I'm coolly polite and physically present, but my heart and spirit are elsewhere. Only once have I confronted a friend who hurt me. And I was ever so rational and polite."

Is Tasha's approach healthy? As a psychologist, I believe that until Tasha can express her negative feelings and her natural assertiveness, she will suffer in silence or she will continue to be "there but not there" in her key relationships. Tasha is merely dealing with her adult relationships the same way she dealt with her family's unhealthy conflict: she is running away.

What predicts how we handle conflict?

Psychologist Kim Bartholomew says our relationships with our parents in early childhood predict how we will respond to conflict in our close, meaningful relationships.[2] Those who were secure in their parents' love and affection have fewer problems in their friendships and romantic attachments than those who were not. These emotionally secure individuals can afford to be assertive in their friendships and romances because they have felt anchored in their parents' love from childhood.

How do emotionally secure women handle conflict? Among the women I interviewed, Heather, a thirty-four-year-old C.P.A. who's a mother at home, is representative of emotionally secure women. Heather describes her relationship with her mother as "very close, but not without its ups and downs." Heather has close relationships with female confidantes, and when conflicts arise in these relationships, she says, "I can't bear unresolved problem situations, and as hard as it is, I will always pursue a resolution. I don't hold grudges, and I don't shrug my shoulders and walk away from a bad situation either."

Heidi, who's expecting her fifth child soon, says she comes from a family of strong, affirming women. She believes problems in relationships can be solved. When she was a manager in human development before coming home, she worked through conflicts with bosses and coworkers. "To perpetuate conflict is degrading," says Heidi, who has very few conflicts with friends. Heidi's approach in her work relationships and friendships is to stress cooperation.

While those who feel anchored in parental love have little trouble being assertive, those who feel emotionally insecure approach their adult relationships with greater tentativeness. Bartholomew suggests that these people have three different ways of coping with conflict in relationships.[3]

First, the *dismissing*. These individuals not only dismiss the importance of their early emotional ties, but they deny or dismiss interpersonal problems. They stuff their negative feelings and try to avoid intimacy. The *fearful*, on the other hand, are afraid to express their negative feelings in relationships, believing if they share their true feelings, that important friend or loved one may just disappear. So they lack assertiveness with them. The *preoccupied* (those who are constantly concerned about their close emotional bonds) often become angry and demanding with others. They try to change others or occupy center stage. The *fearful* and the *preoccupied* are also overly dependent on their adult relationships because they failed to get their dependency needs met in childhood. These individuals don't trust their close relationships and doubt they will last.

I knew I had met a woman capable of *dismissing* her significant attachments when I met Kim. "I don't talk about my mother and I don't do lunch," said this somewhat abrupt woman. And she had said a mouthful without realizing it. What she communicated was her unresolved relationship with her mother as well as her lack of comfort in the intimate experience of a one-on-one conversation with another woman. Kim then added, "I have plenty of friends but none who are particularly close. I function just fine."

Unlike Kim who denies her negative feelings, Deena says she is afraid of conflict. When asked about her parents, she says, "My mother was unpredictable. I was never sure I could count on her, and I never test my friendships." Deena lacks assertiveness, which affects not only her relationships but her work. Recently, her boss took her aside and complimented her on the quality of her work but pointed out her lack of assertiveness.

While Deena is *fearful* to show her anger and say how she feels, Marissa is constantly *preoccupied* with her close attachments. She often gets angry when friends let her down, and she makes demands that some find excessive. When she has vented her anger in the past, some friends have waltzed away.

If we fear we will be rejected or abandoned, it's hard to be assertive in our friendships or love relationships. And yet we sometimes must. Otherwise, we will drift away or demand too much and be eternally disappointed.

Honing conflict resolution skills

Before we look at how to work through conflict, we need to acknowledge that most of us will not choose to speak our truth and confront unless the relationship is central in our lives, professionally or personally. Sometimes it's best to let things pass, particularly if the individual is not someone we work closely with or our husband, child, or close friend. Other times we choose quietly to forgive little injuries. I'm not talking about stuffing or avoiding negative feelings about serious issues, but rather about choosing when to speak and when to overlook or forgive annoyances.

A friend, a Southern Baptist minister, once overheard some parishioners decimate his preaching style as they stood outside his office, not realizing he was there. He elected not to confront them because he says, "Choose the mountains you die on." Another friend says, "I have only so much time and emotional energy. My mother taught me to rise above petty grievances and annoyances and save my energy to work through real issues with those who are significant to me." That's good advice. Besides, we've all had the experience of annoyances evaporating between encounters with important people in our lives.

But if we can't let the grievances go, or if we have conflicts with close friends, we may need to do some truth telling. Then, it's critical to work on the way we view the situation. First, we need to realize that we only see the situation from our own perspective and we don't know what's going on in our friend's heart. And we need to avoid making negative assumptions.

Liz lost a close friend once because of a miscommunication and negative assumptions. Liz and Tanya lived across the street from each other, often confided in each other, and had sons who were best friends. Since both were busy women, Tanya asked Liz to help her give a shower for a friend at work. Liz didn't know Tanya's friend but was willing to help. However, she didn't attend the shower. She assumed if Tanya had wanted her there, she would have asked her to come. Tanya was miffed. She felt Liz had let her down. Besides, it never occurred to her that she would need to formally invite Liz. She assumed Liz knew she was invited.

After the shower, neither woman talked about her disappointment, and both retreated to a distant, polite place. But their friendship was derailed in the process. Today—fifteen years later—Liz still feels bad about what happened.

When we have conflict with a friend, we need to be willing to take the initiative to bring light and reconciliation. Even if we're fearful of rejection, we should ask ourselves if the friendship is valuable enough to try to salvage. If the answer is yes, we can move ahead by going to the other person and saying, "I think we both feel hurt. Let's talk about what just happened." We may have to overcome our pride, but what comfort is pride if we lose a dear friend in the process?

When we finally sit face to face with our friend, it's important to focus on goals that are bigger than any personal differences. We can begin with the following: "Your friendship means a great deal to me. We've shared a lot. And I know you feel hurt just like I do. Can we talk about our feelings, while keeping in mind that our friendship is big enough to survive this?" Once the conversation begins and the heat and the tears come, it's critical to stay focused on the outcome. This will help us weather any storms.

We learn to listen when our friend tells us how she sees the situation. It's often hard to really listen with our hearts, eyes, and ears when we feel we're being portrayed in a negative, distorted fashion. We may get angry, but we need to avoid becoming defensive. It often helps if we can mentally take several steps backward and try to hear the hurt in our friend's voice so that we can empathize with her.

After we've listened and validated her feelings, we then ask if she will listen to us. A word of warning. A friend may get angry if she feels we haven't truly listened but have just waited patiently to recite our litany. It's important to take all the time that's necessary to ensure that our friend has had a chance to tell her story, then ask if she feels she's been heard.

As we tell our story, we indicate that we can understand how she may have perceived the situation in a different way. After all, nobody's perfect. All of us make mistakes daily. So it's okay to admit that we are capable of being selfish and wrong. And it's better to speak about our hurt feelings rather than to point a finger and play the blaming game.

To wrap it up, we need to say we're sorry and ask our friend to forgive us. If she will, we've won back a friend. If she won't, after a time of grieving, we move on and find other close friends. It helps enormously if she asks for forgiveness too. That really clears the air. To maintain a close relationship both need to be willing to ask for and grant forgiveness.

Finally, we need to talk briefly about how to avoid a breach in the relationship the next time. We set some ground rules. We agree not to make negative assumptions or impugn each other's motives. We agree to keep the heat to a minimum and to speak calmly and kindly, avoiding blaming statements. We agree not to allow anger to fester and become resentment and bitterness.

In the process, we'll discover that we keep most of our close friendships and improve our ability to see the world from another's perspective.

Toxins in friendship

In addition to honing conflict resolution skills, we should become aware of toxins in the relationship. Dr. Joel Block says in his book *Friendship: How to Give It, How to Get It* that when relationships flounder, they contain two main toxins.[4] The first is blame. Blame always pulls people apart. And the only antidote for "blame and defensiveness is to assume responsibility for one's feelings, openly look at what part one plays in an unhappy circumstance, and avoid repeating that role in the future."[5]

The second key toxin in any friendship is choking, clinging dependency. Friends control others by "bleeding the life out of them." Overly dependent people need to rediscover their lost strength. It doesn't work, says Block, to overload the friendship and expect undue emotional support. "It is as if self-esteem is not contained within the person but has been passed on to the judgment of others. This kind of person will often feel unable to tolerate being alone since being in his or her own company feels like being in the company of nobody. He will pass countless evenings in meaningless social gatherings, will have endless and pointless conversations with people...and will stay far too late at parties—simply to avoid being alone."[6]

We can't look to friends to fill us up—to provide something we don't possess. If we are too dependent on others, we need to confront our low self-esteem and look for its roots in early childhood. Only when we learn to love ourselves and have compassion for ourselves will we be able to have healthy friendships.

And if we don't keep the toxins out of our significant relationships? When a friend hurts us or ignores us, we begin an inner dialogue. We begin unconsciously to exonerate ourselves and devalue our friend. We tell ourselves how wronged we were and how insensitive our friend is. And the longer we refuse to address the wall between us, the more we fester and withdraw. In the end, our self-righteousness destroys any possibility of reconciliation.

In friendship, as in other lasting relationships, we have to deal with conflicts that refuse to go away. Janice knows she has a friendship that will probably die if she and her friend don't deal with their hurt feelings. Because this friend means a great deal to her, she plans to go to her soon and say, "Let's talk about what's eating us alive." While Janice admits her friend is not very appealing to her right now, she knows this relationship is too important to lose. Janice realizes that once they deal with these grievances, she'll think her friend is wonderful again.

My friend Linda LeSourd Lader, who is the mother of two darling girls and president of the Renaissance Institute, says she learned to deal with conflict in her female friendships in her twenties. After she became a Christian, she worked in Washington, D.C. and lived with a group of women. "That's when I developed friendships where there was a real commitment to each other and when we said there would be no back door in our friendships. If you lock the door in a friendship, you know you can't run from problems and misunderstandings and you have to find a way to work them out."

Linda believes that these committed friendships are a good preparation for marriage. "How can we expect to hang in there and keep our marital commitments if we have had no practice with commitment in our friendships?"

Forever friends

I will always remember when my friend Ros taught me that friendship could not only handle conflict but grow deeper in the process. One day I became angry at Ros but was tentative about expressing my feelings. After all, a husband had just walked away from our relationship. Ros, a therapist, addressed my negative feelings. Then she said something quite remarkable: "I am your friend for life." I was shocked. Here was a relatively new friend making a profound statement. Though I was grateful, I didn't trust her commitment for a long time.

That was twenty-three years ago. In the intervening years I have remarried. Ros has married, had a daughter, gotten divorced. Once, years ago, when she was newly separated and in pain, Don and I flew Ros and Sarah to our house for two weeks. At that time, Ros made another remarkable statement. "I have a family ring in a safe deposit box," she said, "and if ever you need to come to me or I need to see you and Don and there's no money, I'll sell the ring to pay for airline tickets."

I now believe Ros would do just that. During these past twenty years I have experienced deep and loving commitment in my marriage to Don, so abiding friendships and marriages no longer surprise me. After all, David and Jonathan in the Old Testament made a vow to be forever friends. Why shouldn't women, as well as men, be able to remain close, committed friends their whole life long?

Because of what I learned about friendship and conflict resolution from Ros, I could later make a similar commitment to Eleanor.

I tease Eleanor by saying she and I have taken graduate courses in conflict resolution. Although we can laugh about it, Eleanor and I agree that we have had our fair share of arguments. Only my sister, husband, and daughters have required, and received, more emotional energy from me. Why have I given so much to this friendship? Part of it stems from the fact that Eleanor and I founded Home by Choice in 1987 and afterward found ourselves in lock step in two arenas. We not only were close friends but worked together as well.

While working together strengthened our friendship, it also generated greater conflicts and misunderstandings. After all, we had to figure out how to launch an organization, and neither of us had ever done that before! We also had to face the unpleasant fact that we are both pretty territorial and controlling women. So we needed to delineate what Eleanor would handle (administration and management) and what I would control (public relations and printed resources). We discovered along the way that we were control freaks and that in working together we had fewer times just to kick back and talk about personal things. Now organizational "business" often interfered with our richly supportive friendship.

In our forties we occasionally had heated confrontations. When we hit our fifties, we agreed that we were tired of generating so much heat. After all, we're in the heart attack zone now. Lest this sound amusing, the *Washington Times* (March 19, 1994) said that those with heart disease are more than twice as likely to have a heart attack when they get angry because anger increases the heart rate, elevates blood pressure, and aids in clogging the arteries. A study of 1,122 men and 501 women who had survived heart attacks found that their risk of a repeat heart attack was 2.3 times higher during the first two hours after they got angry. Since midlife women become increasingly vulnerable to heart attacks, what Eleanor and I said in jest was based in fact.

So Eleanor and I happily turned down the volume and learned to speak to each other with greater kindness and tact. For several years now this has worked beautifully. Also, we've learned to listen more carefully and to forgive each other again and again. And if we're both overwhelmed by life, we leave a message on the answering machine for the other to think about before we clear the air.

Today my friend and I sit together, having our weekly meeting at an elegant hotel where we sip tea and eat pretzels, all for the grand sum of two dollars each. As the sun streams in the glass ceiling, we share our burdens, our joys, our hearts. I look into my friend's eyes and am grateful for all we've shared and for having learned to survive our conflicts. Invariably, we spend a lot of time laughing together. And as we leave to go our separate ways, both of us admit we feel lighter than when we came.

What are the benefits of resolving conflicts in our meaningful relationships? If we are successful, our friendships become deeper, richer, happier. When we refuse to run away but instead learn to speak the truth in love, we also become anchors to each other in the world of female friendships. That means we become more confident in our relationships with other women.

These seasoned, tested friendships enable us to move out and explore our world, knowing we can take risks because we have enduring relationships to return to. We have those forever friends. And whatever our beginnings, we feel more complete.

12

. . .

Friendship's End

It appears that genuine friendship cannot possibly exist
where one of the parties is unwilling to hear the truth
and the other equally indisposed to speak it.
Cicero, 50 B.C.

My daughter Kristen still remembers the day in seventh grade when Janine ousted her from the lunchroom table. As Kris slid her tray onto the table, Janine looked at the other three girls and said, "We've decided we don't want you to eat with us anymore." This caught Kris by surprise, and when I saw her after school, she was about to cry.

"Do you realize what this means, Mom?" she wailed. "*Everybody* sits together in cliques and I can't simply change tables. This is a catastrophe."

And it was—temporarily. With strong family support, however, Kris rallied to the challenge, sat coolly with her group for a few days, and eventually found new friends who were more accepting. And, not surprisingly, she was never close to Janine and her friends again.

Many of us can remember the anguish of losing friends when we were young. Carlie remembers when she had a falling out with two close friends in fifth grade. Says Carlie, "The reasons for the breach in the relationships were a mystery to me, yet I automatically assumed fault. That caused me to quietly disappear, feeling embarrassed for being rejected."

Marcia, now forty-nine, still remembers when, in seventh grade, her best friend of three years abandoned her for a different group of girls. "That hurt my feelings," says Marcia, "but I didn't say anything. I accepted what I perceived as her rejection and I found another best friend."

Lisa, twenty-seven, remembers the loss of a sixth grade bosom buddy as devastating. She says, "A third girl came into our circle and maneuvered events to break us apart. She encouraged me to talk about my best friend's faults, and when my friend found out about this, she stopped talking to me. We've never been friends since."

Another woman, a thirty-five-year-old nurse, was so tentative in her friendships that when she lost her best friend in childhood, she decided she would never risk closeness to another female again. Blind to the blockage this old hurt has created in her life, she says, "I feel it was resolved, but it still hurts."

One of the saddest stories I've ever heard was told to me by Paula, a woman in her forties. When she was eight, her father walked out and left her at the mercy of her mother's irrational rages. Paula could cope because she depended on her friend Beth for emotional support. She had sleepovers at Beth's house, biked with her, and walked to school with her each day.

Then one day Beth's mother decided that Beth shouldn't be Paula's friend anymore because of Paula's unstable family background. "I understood the mother's point of view," said Paula, "but, oh, how it hurt."

Why do friendships end?

It always hurts to lose best friends, especially in childhood when we feel most vulnerable. But, among the women I interviewed, whether they lost friends in grade school or experienced the rupture of an important relationship in high school, college, or beyond, these experiences are painful indeed. Why did their friendships end?

Sometimes the friend embraced different values or hung out with the wrong crowd. One woman lost her friend in a car accident. Others suddenly discovered that their crowd wasn't popular enough and a best friend moved on to another clique of popular girls.

Even at thirty, Kelly remembers the time she lost both a best friend and a boyfriend. In college, Kelly's best friend began secretly to date Kelly's boyfriend. When Kelly discovered her friend's betrayal, she buried her anger and pretended nothing was wrong. The problem was never discussed, and eventually she and her friend started "hanging out" again. But says Kelly, "Things were not as they were before. A year later the exact same thing happened with another guy. I felt totally betrayed and had a great deal of anger." Again, Kelly chose not to confront her friend, so nothing was ever resolved. These women still see each other occasionally, and at those times the air crackles with tension. "I usually get sarcastic," says Kelly, "and she accuses me of never getting over what happened. Fact is, I will never trust her again."

Betrayal is the bane of friendships. In her book *The Joy of Women's Friendships* Dee Brestin says that while some friendships die because of distance and stress, the most frequent cause of the demise of women's friendships is betrayal.[1] We can put up with a lot of petty selfishness and thoughtlessness, and we can feel sad when our friends move away and seldom call, but we cannot easily stomach betrayal. It wounds too deeply.

Why is betrayal so difficult to handle? When we trust a friend with our secrets, our feelings—ourselves—and she betrays us, we feel violated. We have given the friendship our best, and our best has been trampled on. How can we trust again, we ask ourselves. But of course we must. And most of us eventually do. But we may go into friendships with more realistic expectations as a result.

When we lose a soul mate along the way for whatever reason, we struggle to move on. Michele Paludi, author of *The Psychology of Women*, states that researchers have found the end of female friendships more painful than the end of romantic love.[2] While this may be hard to believe, we must admit we have a lexicon of appropriate behaviors for handling the loss of romantic, heterosexual relationships. But how do we handle the loss of a best friend?

In their book *Bittersweet: Facing Up to Feelings of Love, Envy and Competition in Women's Friendships*, Susie Orbach and Luise Eichenbain observe that people commiserate when a woman loses a boyfriend, but nobody "rushes around with a hot dinner or evening entertainment when a best girlfriend is lost."[3] Consequently, these therapists believe that the loss of an important female friend leaves us "temporarily fragile." Why? They say we unconsciously transfer our feelings about the mother/daughter relationship to the friendship. Consequently, we want to "be cared for," but at the same time we're afraid we'll be judged harshly for having needs."[4] The loss, then, of a close friendship reopens early wounds.

When I lost a best friend six years ago, I ran to the one person I felt would understand—my husband, Don. One day when I was feeling particularly low, Don met me at a local coffee shop. Astute man that he is, he had seen the rupture coming and knew how much I had invested in this important friendship. As I looked toward the door, I saw Don walk in, carrying a long, white florist's box. "Here," he said, smiling. "I know how much she meant to you, and this is a token of my love." Inside were a dozen, long-stemmed, red roses.

Warning signs

Since friendship's end is so painful to women, how can we recognize when a friendship is on the skids? What are the warning signs?

First, there's an increasing emotional distance which, if not addressed, eventually results in a physical distance. If we're sensitive to our friend's body language, we become aware of decreased eye contact. She leans away from us rather than into the conversation, or sits with arms crossed in a closed position. Her tone of voice may also change. Once warm and enthusiastic, now she's chilly and distant. Or she seems preoccupied. "I can always tell when you're mad at me," said one woman to her best friend. "You pull away, and your voice becomes flat and cold."

In addition to body language, we notice that our friend isn't as open as she used to be. She listens politely to the private thoughts and struggles we put on the table, but she is more guarded than usual and doesn't share her deepest concerns anymore. If we're astute and aware, we sense that she's gradually withdrawing her emotional investment from the relationship.

Later on we begin to notice that our friend doesn't call as often as she used to or she takes too long to return our calls. She's too busy to meet for lunch or dinner. She, who always had time for us before, is truly sorry but right now she's just too strung out. We need to understand, she says.

We can ask our friend if she's angry and, depending on how important the relationship is to her, she may share her feelings. Then resolution begins to be possible. If, however, she has already decided the relationship just isn't worth the effort, we can knock on the door of her heart as loudly as we wish, but to no avail. Our friend has simply gone away.

When is it okay to walk away?

Sometimes both parties decide to withdraw amicably from a friendship. As Eva was considering divorce from her husband of twenty years, she began to drift away from her old friends who decried divorce to new friends who were more tolerant of her lifestyle change.

"I felt her slowly disappear," says Ann, a friend of fifteen years. "It was progressive, over a period of years actually. First, I felt less valuable as a mentor in her life. We were both photographers. I was established; she wanted to develop her skills. As Eva's values began to change, she found other mentors. That hurt. One day it dawned on me that the woman I enjoyed and loved for years no longer existed. In her place was someone I no longer knew or understood. So there were no fights. Not even a confrontation. We just stopped calling and seeing each other."

Ann confesses that some days she misses Eva. "There is a hole in my life that Eva used to fill." But the death of their friendship was gradual, and both women saw the end coming over a period of years. Sadly, neither took steps to resuscitate the dying patient.

Could they have revived their friendship? Perhaps. But what had occurred was a progressive change in lifestyle and values. And having similar values is pretty basic in all relationships.

When can a friendship be saved?

However, when the changes in the relationship aren't so profound, it is possible to breathe new life into a waning friendship. If we can identify the downward trend and any negative behavior early enough, and take steps to overcome it, the friendship may be able to heal itself and survive.

Steve Duck, the scientific guru of relationships, says there are identifiable stages in the dissolution of relationships, beginning with unhappiness with a partner, confronting the partner, telling others about the relationship distress, and finally the "grave dressing stage"—burying the friendship and going on. Duck says repair is possible at each stage if both partners want it.[5] In friendship, as in marriage, it is not enough for one party to want the relationship to continue. Both partners have to become reinvested in the relationship, and even then, hard work and fits and starts lie ahead.

Yvonne sits on the sofa recounting the death of her friendship with Vicky. "We had been buddies for years, helping each other through the loss of jobs and boyfriends. I thought I could always count on her when the chips were down. Then we had a major falling-out and let it fester.

"We went to England to visit Vicky's relatives and had an accident in a rented car. Vicky refused to pay any of the damages because I had been driving. I fumed silently and buried my feelings for the rest of the trip, and we pretended to ignore the situation. The more time passed, the angrier I got, and the more Vicky—sensing my mood—withdrew.

"Soon she started dating a new man and we seldom saw each other. When I finally went to her to address the problem, it was too late. She didn't need me anymore and I felt devastated."

Yvonne adds quietly, "I lost one of the best friends I ever had."

Grieving friendship's end

As Yvonne found when she tried to revive an important friendship, it is not always possible to do so. At that point—when we know in our gut that the friendship is over—how do we deal with the angst?

First, we grieve. And grieving friendship's end is a process that may take weeks, months, or even years. A lot depends on how the relationship ends. If both parties move to other locales or simply drift away, the loss is muted. But if one friend rejects the other, the pain can be great.

As we have said before, the way a woman responds to such a loss will also depend on how secure she is in general. If a woman has strong, secure relationships, she is far less likely to lose a best friend in the first place. But even if she should lose a best friend, she believes she is intrinsically a decent and lovable woman and as such will find other close friends. Often this confident, secure woman has a coterie of friends, so the loss of one, even a close one, isn't so devastating.

This is not the case for the woman who has had a parent die or walk out, or who has had boyfriends or a husband leave. When this woman loses a best friend, the new loss touches on the pain of old losses. Said a colleague, "Some of us have a lifelong bucket of pain we carry around, and each new loss reminds us of that." Also she may have fewer friends to begin with. The result? She may grieve for some time and feel overly responsible for the friendship's demise. She may also get quite depressed, especially in the beginning. These women are simply more vulnerable to friendship's end than those who had secure beginnings.

As we grieve, it helps to share our pain with another close friend, a husband, a grown daughter. We will need our comforters—those who will put their arms around us, hold us, empathize with us, and help us learn from the loss of this meaningful relationship.

Grief isn't ever pleasant, but it is necessary. And in some mysterious way known only to God, we grow when our hearts are broken. We become less judgmental, less self-righteous, less convinced that our way is best. If we allow ourselves to feel and express our pain, we do become more compassionate in the end.

As we grieve honestly, we learn about the power of our human bonds. God has created us to be able to love husbands, children, friends. And the loss of any special person is deeply and keenly felt. But that is as it should be. To be able to love means we may also be rejected.

And then? We can suffer and grow, or retreat. We can wall off our hearts and post a sign that says, "Scale it if you dare." But the result is that we will be lonely on the other side of the wall. I once told a client who had been deeply hurt, "You can stay on your side of the wall and insist that others scale the wall and walk on glass to reach you, but very few will ever do that. Better to let God heal your wounded heart and with His help dismantle your wall."

One way to avoid erecting a wall is through writing or journaling. Several of my clients have found this a helpful exercise in coming to terms with the past or processing fresh pain.

The sheer act of writing externalizes what's going on inside and helps exorcise the pain. I once heard the well-known psychiatrist Murray Bowen say that clients who wrote about their painful relationships got better faster. As a writer, I know that writing is an excellent tool for unearthing emotions and for making sense out of what has happened to us.

When a deep friendship ends, we mourn. We get angry. We confide in another friend, or a husband, or our mother. We go to God and tell Him how troubled we are. We try to tease apart our responsibility for the failed relationship.

Facing friendship's end also involves honest assessment of our own relational skills, and it necessitates seeing our friends as imperfect and friendship as less than ideal. "Close friendships require a sense of self, an interest in other people, empathy and loyalty and commitment," writes Judith Viorst. "They also require the letting go—the necessary loss—of some of our fantasies of ideal friendship."[6]

But as we let go, we grow. We let go of fantasies, yes. And sometimes we must let go of a special friend. And the next time around we find we can be better friends—wiser perhaps and less demanding—than we were before.

13

· · ·

When Men
Aren't Enough

Husbands were made to be talked to.

It helps them concentrate their minds on what they're reading.

C. S. Lewis

Six in the morning. The neighborhood is still shrouded in moist shadows, but Jan and Linda are dressed in wind suits, out for their morning walk. As they walk, they talk about their marriages, children, and work. Both regard this as an energizing ritual before they face family breakfasts and part-time jobs.

"Do you know what Tom said when I told him I wanted to finish college rather than continue working at the bank? He said I didn't need a college degree. I could find a full-time job now managing a restaurant!" says Jan, feigning indignation.

Jan feels that her husband didn't hear her the preceding night when she shared her dreams with him. She, a mother of four who dropped out of nursing school to marry Tom, wants desperately to finish college and become a professional now that their kids are older. And she's angry because Tom failed to understand her feelings.

Linda listens to Jan's frustration and in a gentle, teasing way reminds her that only three days ago she said her husband was wonderful. Both laugh and begin working on the issue at hand: Tom feels threatened and Jan feels vulnerable about her dream. As cars whiz by, Jan says with exaggerated emphasis, her hands on her hips, "Oh, you *always* let Tom off the hook. And you always make me analyze things." Linda smiles, knowing that for all her protestations, Jan wants to understand herself and her marriage better.

As they walk along, both women occasionally touch each other's shoulder or stop periodically to face each other and gesticulate wildly, their voices rising and their words punctuated by laughter.

A sun-dried, seventy-year-old man wearing a neon orange ski hat strolls by, smiles at the women, and says, "You two look like you're doing ballet."

And so they are. These friends are "dancing in synchrony" as they listen, encourage, and challenge each other's viewpoint.

Do men dance with us in the same way? Can they meet our emotional needs completely, or is the female ballet as essential to a woman's sense of well-being as the male-female tango?

In my conversations with women I hear a steady refrain:

• "Our husbands just don't understand us."

• "If men got PMS, all the researchers in the world would be investigating cures."

• "Menopause is not a figment of the female imagination."

• "Men just don't get as excited about the really important things in life–relationships, shopping, and cappuccino."

What women say about men

In my interviews with women one of the questions I asked them was, "Do you feel there are things you can share with other women you cannot share with your husbands?" While a number of women said emphatically they could share everything with their husbands, other women felt they were best understood in some areas by their own sex. Here's a sampling of their comments:

Mary Ellen, thirty-four: "It's easier for me to read a book or an article about a unique idea and then have a deep conversation about it with another woman than it is for me to discuss it with my husband."

Nancy, fifty: "I share most things with my husband, but I don't feel he always understands where I'm coming from and exactly what I mean, like many women do. Maybe it's the fact that women have been there. Also, I'm a feeler and many of my female friends are. My husband is not into feelings. He wants to solve or fix my problems. I need someone just to listen and encourage me to think through things."

Marlene, forty-eight: "Women tend to be better listeners. My husband's personality and mine are opposites. He's logical, perfectionistic, and methodical, and I'm more creative and spontaneous. He and I differ on what we think is crucial. So while he's a good balance for my weaknesses, I turn to female friends for understanding in certain areas."

Carlie, forty-one: "Absolutely. Simply put, men, even someone as sensitive and open as my husband, just don't get a lot of things. Or they don't appreciate the humor or significance in the way another woman or a mother does. So sometimes it's just more fun or satisfying to share certain things with my women friends."

Betty, forty-seven: "My husband has a limit on how much verbiage can go into his ears at any one time. So I'm careful about the quantity of words I speak. While I share more with him than anyone else, I do have a female friend who's a good sounding board for petty marital irritations."

What I discovered in talking to these women is underscored by a 1989 Gallup Poll, which found that for both sexes, a best friend is likely to be of the same sex. Eighty-one percent of the women polled, and 69 percent of the men, preferred same-sex best friends. Among the married, only 17 percent of the men and 13 percent of the women considered a spouse to be a best friend.

What do men uniquely give us?

While the majority of American women communicate better with their own sex and look to their own sex for a best friend, the *New Woman* survey found that married women are generally happier than single women. Among married women, 71 percent said their husband was their biggest supporter. Sixty percent felt they could always count on their husband or boyfriend, and 58 percent said their husbands loved them most and gave them confidence.

Support. Trust. Love. Confidence. These are powerful gifts that men give us. And this does not take into account all those areas outside the emotional arena: protection, financial support, fathering. Some men feel women view these areas far too casually. This was evident in conversations I had with several men in preparing to write this chapter. Realizing they are combating a myth in the nineties—that men aren't really necessary—here's what they said:

"Women need men for emotional and financial support," said the fifty-year-old husband of a traditional wife and mother. "I know men get a bad rap because they sometimes are unable to meet all of their wives' emotional needs, but most work at it, and many of us do a pretty good job. Also, the financial support that a husband and father provides is not inconsequential. Just look at what happens in fatherless families. Welfare rolls swell."

Several husbands were keenly aware that their wives relied on them for psychological and physical protection. "My wife knows I set boundaries with her mother," said one husband. "Her mom isn't critical and demanding when I'm around. Also, my wife says she sleeps better when I'm home and doesn't feel as secure when I'm away on a business trip."

Men also provide women with the possibility of sexual fulfillment. Through the sexual intimacy we share with husbands, we come into our own as women. "My husband makes me feel like a woman," said one woman after a romantic fling away from the kids. And that sexual intimacy with a husband creates a bond like no other.

In addition, the men I talked to recognize their crucial role in fathering their children. They know they are essential in their sons' and daughters' achievement and self-esteem. Without being social scientists, they understand that much of both white and black teenage crime is the result of fatherless families.

"I know my wife needs me to set limits for my teenagers," said one forty-five-year-old husband. "She just can't get through to our 6'4" son at times, and I protect her against our daughter's surliness and disrespect."

These off-the-cuff observations are supported by decades of scholarly research. Writer Karl Zinsmeister stated in a speech on fathering given to the Family Research Council in June 1992 that since time immemorial fathers have played critical roles in their children's lives as teachers, disciplinarians, and as the parent who establishes gender.

A world without men is impossible to envision. Men provide the challenge of a different world view. Their bodies, their perceptions of life and relationships, and their orientation to life are different from ours. And as such, men enrich our lives greatly. Men are *other*. Women are *same*.

So let's celebrate the differences between men and women, knowing we will always need men in our lives as fathers, brothers, friends, providers, husbands, and mentors.

My husband, Don, has been a mentor to me in the professional area throughout our marriage. He was the one who suggested I fulfill a lifelong dream and write a book during the first year of our marriage. Each night Don listened as I read the pages I had written, and he encouraged me to continue. He has also made editorial comments on all the books and articles I've published.

Later when the girls were in high school, it was Don who suggested I fulfill a second personal dream and pursue a Ph.D. at Georgetown. When I remonstrated because of self-doubt and anxiety, he said, "You can do it." His approach to anything I've attempted has been, "You can do it." And when I passed my orals, this man stood in line at the DMV to purchase a congratulatory license tag for me that read "DR MOM." For all the productive things I've done these past twenty years, I owe a great deal to my husband's love and encouragement.

We can't get along without men in our lives, nor would we want to. Even so, they cannot provide all we need of love, friendship, and understanding. We will always need the communion of other women, and this will help us become better wives and mothers.

When aren't men enough?

For one thing, in their attempt to help us deal with problems, men focus on solutions, not feelings. Charmaine says that when she went through an exceptionally difficult experience at work, every time her husband and she discussed it "the focus of our conversations was strategizing what to do about the situation. By contrast, when I told my friend Jena what happened, she cried. I was really moved because she had instantly picked up on how hurt I was and responded instinctively."

Deborah Tannen, a Georgetown University professor of linguistics and the current guru of conversational styles between men and women, confirms this male/female difference. In her best-selling book *You Just Don't Understand,* Tannen describes the differences between her husband and herself as they approach the conversational world. She says of her husband:

> It is a continual source of pleasure to talk to him. It is wonderful to have someone I can tell everything to, someone who understands. But he doesn't always see things as I do, doesn't always react to things as I expect him to. And I often don't understand why he says what he does.

> Having done the research that led to this book, I now see that my husband was engaging the world in a way that many men do: as an individual in a hierarchical social order in which he was either one-up or one-down. In this world, conversations are negotiations in which people try to achieve and maintain the upper hand if they can and protect themselves from others' attempts to put them down and push them around. Life, then, is a contest, a struggle to preserve independence and avoid failure.

> I, on the other hand, was approaching the world as many women do: as an individual in a network of connections. In this world conversations are negotiations for closeness in which people seek to give confirmation and support, to reach consensus.[1]

The images that come to mind as I read Tannen's words were suggested by psychologist Ruthellen Josselson. She describes male development as hierarchical, using the image of the pyramid, and female development as interconnected, like a web.[2] Throughout their lives men are concerned with ascendancy and self-protection in conversation and life, but women make themselves vulnerable in order to anchor their lives in relationships with men, children, and other women.[3] And part of the way we make ourselves vulnerable in our relationships is through conversations.

Give us words

"Words, words, words," said one exasperated writer. "My wife came to me this morning and said she wants *words*. Now I know she doesn't want just any old words; she wants carefully chosen words that she calls 'intimate.'" This man, who can supply words for scholarly books and articles, struggles with good humor and no little frustration to find the words that will satisfy his wife.

This husband is right: not just any words will do. A woman wants words that recognize her feelings, for these words show that her husband cares. She also wants her husband to display his vulnerabilities, to show her his heart—"to unzip his chest," as one lawyer said to her uncomprehending husband. Some men can do this on demand, but many cannot.

The sexes and words

Tannen says part of the reason men and women have trouble understanding each other is that they use words differently. Men engage in "report-talk" and women in "rapport talk."[4] For men, talk is information. For women, it's interaction. Women see conversation as a vehicle to establish and maintain connections. "From childhood, men learn to use talking as a way to get and keep attention."[5] Tannen believes they are more comfortable speaking publicly to strangers than they are speaking privately to the love of their life.

Men use words competitively, to maintain control. I have a male friend who exhibits this in spades. A university professor, he is extremely knowledgeable in two arenas—psychology and theology. Bright and aggressive, he will control conversation in a group for an entire evening. His tactic for keeping the floor is quite effective. After he has talked for a while and he senses that someone is about to interrupt, he speeds up, uses connectors like "and" or "while" that he accentuates, and begins a different topic or aspect of the former subject. Conversations with this man are like stock car races. One feels like a race car driver, ever trying to pass him while he insists on speeding up and staying out front. This kind of thing rarely happens when two women talk.

For women, "telling things is a way to show involvement, and listening is a way to show interest and caring."[6] Sadly, as wives or girlfriends, we often feel our husbands or boyfriends don't care about us because they'd rather read the newspaper or watch pro football on TV than talk to us. And many couples fight about these different needs, blaming each other and feeling misunderstood.

Don has never lacked words, but we still have our conversational differences. Early in our marriage, when I struggled to understand and articulate my feelings, my rash, forty-year-old husband would say, "Get to the bottom line." Instead, I would get angry. How dare he be so rude! And around we'd go. Don has since been schooled by the women in his life, at home and at the office, to listen patiently. While he enjoys listening to the girls and me talk about our feelings, he is also grateful I have close female friends. He admits he cannot understand why we allow each other to continually circle the mountain, discharging emotion, before finally arriving at the top hours later. He cannot believe women do not notice the repetition.

He used to say, "You've said that twice before."

And I used to respond, "But I need to say it three times, and I need you to listen." This is apparently a male/female difference in conversational style.

What's the solution? We need to understand and accept the fact that men are different, not only sexually but conversationally, and cease trying to turn them into women. Men need to learn not to count the repetitions, and women, to get to the point more quickly. As we live together and sharpen each other, flint against flint, we do change.

Hormonal crazies

Just as husbands may never fully understand the positive impact empathetic words have on our marriages and sense of well-being, they probably can't truly understand the enormous impact our hormones have on our lives. Women often turn to each other for emotional support as they negotiate those passages of life that are uniquely female: having and mothering children, PMS, menopause. In leading menopause groups I often witness firsthand the enormous relief that comes when women listen to each other talk about their menopausal symptoms. Suddenly they are not alone. They feel normal. "I'm not crazy because I feel like a 'cat on a hot tin roof.' I'm not ready for an institution because I have fantasies of running away for a while." Women who come to the first meeting worried and uptight often leave relaxed, less anxious. They have just experienced that wonderful feeling that comes from the company of women.

In this particular area, men can't provide the understanding women crave. I remember a husband who called the mental health clinic where I work. When the scheduler asked about his wife's problem, he replied that she was suffering from "mental pause." Most midlife women can attest to the truth of that, and many of us feel our male gynecologists give short shrift to PMS and the mood swings caused by the erratic hormones of the premenopausal stage.

Of course, many husbands try to be sympathetic, and some increase their understanding over time. Said one enlightened husband, "Raising three daughters has been a profound experience for me. I've learned PMS is not a figment of the female imagination. I feel that monthly drop in self-esteem and surge of crabbiness in my very core. Menopause? That's a time either to head for the hills or form a male survivors group."

Menopause is hard on many husbands, and they, like their wives, need accurate information and moral support. And it's a time when every woman should have a working relationship with a gynecologist who will answer her questions fully.

And those women who have a difficult midlife transition could profit from a support group. Facing bodily changes, losing hair, struggling with adolescents, aging parents, the empty nest, and estrogen—these are issues no woman should face alone. Said one woman, "My friends have literally gotten me through menopause. As I've laughed with them about what I've been going through, I've felt so much better emotionally. If I can laugh, I don't cry."

Understanding the men in our lives

A final thought. Although other women often are more articulate and empathetic listeners, we need to make sure we still give men a chance. Charmaine raised an interesting issue when she said, "I think some women go a little too far with this idea that women fill a need their husbands can't, so they quit trying to develop emotional intimacy with their husbands. Being friends with women is, in a way, the path of least resistance, and being friends with our husbands is more challenging."

She's right. It's often easier to bear our hearts to women we're close to. And for lots of reasons it's sometimes tougher with the men in our lives. But if we want our marriages to prosper, we can never cease trying to better understand our husbands, even as we take pressure off the marriage occasionally by talking with our female friends.

While some wives I have talked with had emotional as well as sexual intimacy in their marriages from the start, others said they had grown closer to their mates over the years. "We've learned to listen, to share deeply," said one who had been married thirty years. "It hasn't been easy, but the rewards have been worth all the effort."

My experiences in my own marriage and in my work as a therapist have taught me that we need to ensure we are creating the kind of milieu that allows men to open their hearts. It's hard for any man to take off his armor if the arrows are whizzing by. One man, in attempting to explain his maleness, said, "Look past the words, the aggressiveness, the bravado. Each man was once a little boy, and somewhere in that male breast that little boy lives."

And if that little boy was not emotionally close to his mother when he was very young, he may have trouble sharing his feelings later on with his wife and children. But a committed marriage provides a structure for men, as well as women, to change, to grow. And being empathetic and responsive to a husband is one of the best ways to encourage him to respond in kind.

Throughout our lives we need both—close, confiding relationships with males and females. We need to listen both to male and female voices.

◆ ◆ ◆

Why Men Aren't Enough—the Man's Explanation

Dr. Brenda Hunter has written a serious, important book that will be read by literally thousands of women across the United States, mainly because that is one of the mystifying things that women love to do—read books about what it means to be a woman. According to a recent scientific study, conducted while I had a cup of coffee at Borders bookstore, women are approximately 473 times more likely to spend money on "who am I and how did I get this way?" books than men are. In fact, on any given day when the Gothic romance section is overcrowded, this ratio expands to 642 to 1.

As part of my scientific research, I visited the "who am I and how did I get this way?" section one day, taking the understandable precautions of donning an Alan Alda disguise and tucking a well-worn, tear-stained copy of *The Bridges of Madison County* under my arm. Astounding sight: shelf after shelf of books about women and their mothers, women and their sisters, women and their second cousins once-removed. On another shelf—women and pain, women and misery, women and love, women in pain in love, women in love with pain. A section on women and their bodies: love your body (ages twenty to thirty), learning to live with your body (ages thirty to forty), how to ignore your body (postforty). One entire wall was devoted to menopause. (Note to women: if you ever want to clear the room of all men in about fifteen seconds, loudly mention the word *menopause*. In a pinch, *hysterectomy* will do almost as well.)

Men don't read these kinds of books for a very good reason: the basic question "who am I and how did I get this way?" just doesn't interest men because:

1. we already know who we are;

2. we're late for work and don't have time to think about it;

3. the words "Dallas Cowboys" don't appear anywhere in the sentence.

Chances are, if the book jacket doesn't have a picture of a tool on the cover, men aren't going to mess around with it.

Nevertheless, all married men have sincerely wrestled at length with the second most important question that troubles women, to wit, "Why doesn't my husband meet all my needs?" In fact, most of us wrestle with this question every night in bed because at the precise moment we are dropping off to sleep our wives gently remind us in their loving, sensitive, nurturing way that we sure aren't getting the job done in the "true intimacy" department.

I am pleased to report, after years of scientific research, that men have now discovered the answer to this question, an answer which has two parts:

1. Just when we think we have met all known expectations of our loving wives and are looking forward to a good night's sleep, our wives introduce new, previously unmentioned, unmet needs that are causing them to be very unhappy and not "in the mood." (In international negotiations, this phenomenon is known as "moving the goalposts.")

2. The second part is known in science as a true fact, the first hints of which can be found in the story of Adam and Eve. Although everyone knows the story of Adam and Eve, recent discovery of ancient manuscripts has added a few new details that are related here for the first time.

Adam, the first man, noble creature, lived in the Garden of Eden where he was very busy. After naming all the animals, teaching the monkeys the difference between a forward pass and a lateral, and visiting the hardware store hundreds of time, Adam got lonely, probably because ESPN had not been invented yet. When God saw that Adam was lonely, he took action and caused Adam to fall into a deep slumber.

While Adam was sleeping, Eve arrived from another planet on a spaceship she had named "Adam's Rib" for reasons she never explained. When Adam awoke, there she stood—God's most beautiful and wonderful creation, the first woman. As Adam gazed in rapt wonder, Eve spoke her first words—"Can we talk?" The musical tones of Eve's voice still resonating thrillingly in his ears, Adam could only reply yes.

Eve quickly pulled out the Spring 7152 B.C. issue of *Southern Living*, turned to page 49, and showed Adam the floor plan for a 4BR traditional home, with nursery, sunroom, wraparound veranda, and two-car garage. "Build me this house, honey," said Eve, and the first romance had begun.

That night, as Adam contentedly drifted off to sleep in the arms of his new wife, Eve was moved to probe the depths of her new love and establish a firm foundation of intimacy. She asked, "If I die first, how long will it be before you marry again?"

The next day they went to the mall to buy furniture and drapes, and Eve shared with Adam her hopes and dreams about having a great room added to the back of the house. That was when Adam first began to suspect that Eve was from another planet.

Over the ensuing years, unassailable evidence has amassed to support the widely accepted view among men that women are from another planet. For example, women dress to meet the approval of other women, not to impress men. No man, of course, dresses to please another man.

Women talk about things as a means of finding out what they think; men think issues through before they speak in order to say exactly what they think.

Male and female approaches to problems are widely divergent. Women talk about problems or conflict in order to sort out their feelings—"How did that make you feel, dear?" Men assess the situation and offer a solution. Men want to know "What did you do?"

Men build; women make nests.

Men buy stuff; women shop.

Men have buddies; women need true friends.

These differences are clearly the result of origins on different planets. The primary commonality I have discovered is this: on a crowded metro train, a woman prefers to sit down beside another woman. So does the average man.

So, given different planetary origins, it should not be a surprise that women have to seek out their own kind in order to have many of their basic emotional needs met. (The well-adjusted man accepts this situation. He relishes it. He wishes she would stop asking so many questions and just go see her friends.) The important thing for both sexes to accept is the necessity for mutual understanding and respect.

So, the next time that male-female conflict arises in the home, the man can reassure himself by remembering, "She's from another planet." The woman, of course, will be thinking, "Men are so shallow. I'm glad that women are deep. We're superior." Herein lies the basis for contentedness.

Scott McMichael is a lieutenant colonel in the army and is the author of a book on Russia. He is married to Anne-Marie, and they live with their three children in Vienna, Virginia.

14

• • •

Mentors:
Passing the Torch

My commitment to mentoring came from my early years as a

young professional. Many offered criticism. Few offered help.

I vowed if I survived I would help others

in their spiritual and professional journeys.

Dr. Patricia Ennis

ost of my knowledge about womanliness and motherhood has
come from books," wrote Beth Sharpton for *Virtue* magazine in
June 1993. "But I long for a friend who has persevered through
child raising and other stages of life who will teach me through her example
and experience."

What does Sharpton long for this mentor to teach her? Swahili or
Greek or gourmet cooking or hang gliding? No, she needs help with the
basics: how to handle her toddlers, how to nurture her own spirituality, how
to care for a home. Sharpton admits she needs someone older and wiser to
teach her how to balance the many competing demands in her life—like
the need for exercise and the need for time for private pursuits like music
and reading. Beth says she is "starved" for a relationship with a mentor. She
adds poignantly, "I feel emptiness where there should be a relationship
between women in different stages of life."

Beth Sharpton is not alone. That she touched a nerve is evident from
the responses *Virtue* received. Several months after Sharpton's honest and
vulnerable article, *Virtue* printed many of these responses in the "Letters to

the Editor" section of the magazine. Wrote one woman from Beaverton, Oregon: "I've discovered there are far more women desiring to be mentored than are willing to make this commitment." Another wrote from Vista, California: "I have searched for this relationship for many years and have been disappointed. I talked with women I met for the first time—also the last—and wondered if I expected more than they could give or if there is something about the way I approach them that makes them not want a relationship with me."

Another who had been unsuccessful in finding a mentor added: "Is it the responsibility of the younger woman to seek out the older?… We desperately want and need their love and friendship." She then adds despairingly, "We are convinced they do not care about us."

Along with these poignant letters were others from women who had been successful in finding mentors. One from Tucson, Arizona, wrote that her mentor had challenged her to grow by asking probing questions and by being honest with her when others weren't. She said, "The ugliest parts of me have been exposed, accepted and re-labeled with positive words. At times I ran from this person, yet felt drawn to her because she helped me see that I neither had to be perfect or positive. Only real."

After working with young mothers for over a decade, I can confirm Sharpton's perception that most younger women long for a relationship with an older, more experienced woman. In 1984 I spoke to a group of younger mothers at a church in Seattle, Washington, when I was promoting my second book. As I finished and began packing up my papers, a woman in her early thirties walked up, holding the hand of her blond, cherubic three-year-old daughter. She said wearily, "I have really tried to find an older woman to become involved in my life, and I have even looked in this church. But I haven't found anyone." Then she added, "Where are they? Where are all those Titus Two moms who are supposed to help us become better wives and mothers?"

Where have all the mentors gone?

Where are they indeed? As I have listened to younger women ask this question repeatedly over the years, I have in turn asked older women how they feel about nurturing the younger generation. Some have smiled and said, "Grandma's on a career track." This is often true for women in their forties and fifties. Now that they no longer have to juggle career and children, they hit their fifties at a dead run, funneling all their drive and energy into a career. "I no longer feel torn between work and family as I did in my late twenties and thirties," says Zoe, a midlife graphics designer. "As a consequence, I have become much more productive in all phases of my life."

They discover that postmenopausal zest so often written about. And even when their daughters live close by, these daughters often find they have to schedule time well in advance so they can see their busy mothers.

Other midlife women who may have worked only part-time or not at all are thrilled to be finally out of the house. Said one woman in her forties who stayed home longer than most because her youngest child was handicapped, "It's my time now. I know my daughters want to see me more often, but I'm in graduate school and I love it. Besides, I had to wait for my time far too long."

Sometimes women of a certain age who don't go back to school or to work elect to focus all their nurturing capacities on their own extended families. Once when I spoke on passing the torch to the younger generation at a luncheon in Asheville, North Carolina, a woman came up to me and said, "Thanks, Brenda, but no thanks. I have no time or interest in nurturing any younger women unless they're members of my own family." With that, she turned on her heel and walked away.

In addition to pursuing careers or focusing on their own families, many women fail to act as mentors because they simply can't believe that nineties professionals have anything to learn from them. These women, particularly those who have stayed home to rear their children, often suffer from low self-esteem because the media has nailed them as Donna Reed. For the past thirty years women in America have been told that personality development and personal growth are to be found only in the marketplace. The explicit media message has been that any woman who devotes her time and energies to caring for family first is wasting her life. Is it any wonder that a woman who opted for home and hearth feels that she has little to offer those fast-track careerists who are coming home?

The irony is that often these careerists are the very women who long for relationships with the Donna Reeds of America. I've had numerous bright, articulate, nineties professionals tell me they desire relationships with women who put family first. They believe these moms can round out their perceptions of life at home. These women can teach them how to structure their days efficiently, care for their spiritual and intellectual needs, rear children on-site, and relate to single earner husbands.

So most of us need mentoring, whether we are in our twenties or fifties. But what is involved in being a mentor?

What is a mentor?

Webster's defines a mentor as a "trusted counselor and guide," yet a mentor is much more than that. She is a pathfinder who may be ten to twenty years older, or she may simply be a peer who has experienced the life task that lies before us. She has scaled the mountain we intend to climb. She comes down from a camp farther up the mountain and says, "Come on up. The air and the view are wonderful here. Watch those rocks, but follow the path you see on your right." As a guide, this pathfinder sharpens our skills, enlarges our perceptions, and gives us the confidence that, like her, we too can climb the mountain and conquer the obstacles ahead.

A mentor befriends, teaches, and inspires. Through her involvement with a younger woman, a mentor shares from the abundant wealth of her life: her knowledge about marriage, career, children, and interpersonal relationships. She encourages the younger woman to learn new skills, whether in her career or her marriage. As my friend Ree says, "A mentor comes alongside, puts her arm around you, and says, 'You can do it.'" As a mentor shares openly from her life, speaking of her failures as well as her successes, the younger woman is the richer for it.

Sometimes a mentor shares her faith in the middle of a personal crisis. Jenna, a twenty-three-year-old, speaks about what her friendship with Peggy has meant to her. Peggy, who is in her mid sixties, has beaten breast cancer twice and now faces the toughest battle of her life: lung cancer. Jenna, whose own mother has had breast cancer, says, "Peggy has shown incredible optimism and courage in facing the recurrence of cancer. Since I am at high risk for breast cancer, Peggy is a powerful witness to me. Her approach is 'let go and let God.'" Jenna adds, "Peggy is an example of someone whose indefatigable faith in God has grown through a difficult and frightening experience."

Mentors in the workplace

When I was reviewing the research on mentoring, I found that most of the work addresses mentoring in the professions (law, medicine) or in the corporate world. Christina, a twenty-four-year-old writer, has a mentor who helped her land her current job as a speech writer after they worked together at a nonprofit organization. Christina looks to Karen, a seasoned politico, for advice on interpersonal and work relationships. Aware of Karen's career development, contacts, and salary increases, Christina plots her own growth in the workplace.

Belle Rose Ragins says that for career advancement, women need to find mentors who are "higher ranking, influential, senior organization members with advanced experience and knowledge who are committed to providing upward mobility and support to a protégé's professional career."[1] Ragins adds that mentors usually sign on for the long term, filter inside information to their protégés, and act as a buffer between the organization and the individual. Mentors, in sum, build self-confidence and provide career guidance and emotional support. It's naive, says Ragins, to assume that competence in the workplace is enough.

Even though women at work need mentoring, they are not assertive in finding mentors. One study found that only 19 percent were actively looking for a mentor.[2] So women in the workplace need mentors to help them become their most successful selves. And if they fail to find a mentor? The evidence is that they are not as successful in their careers as they otherwise might have been.

Mentoring during transitions

Jill, a thirty-four-year-old attorney with two small children, speaks of those desperate feelings she had when she first came home. "I don't like to admit that many of my feelings of self-worth were tied to my career, but they were. I hated that first party I attended when I told a man I'd just met, 'I stay home with my children,' and he turned on his heel and walked away!"

Jill currently needs a mentor, perhaps someone like Carlie. Carlie, who used to work as a tax attorney for a law firm, took an extended, six months' leave after the birth of her first child, Peter. "I stayed home long enough to fall in love with him," she says. Now a mother of three boys, who are eleven months, three years old, and six years old, Carlie loves being home with her sons. "They're so cute right now," she says, "I hate to leave them, even for a few days." During her years at home Carlie has founded Mothers' First, a local support group, and she has worked with Lawyers at Home, a Washington, D.C. advocacy group.

"Did you see the playground I helped raise funds for?" she asks as I visit her lovely home. While Carlie's first priority is her family, she has used her considerable skills in her community and on national TV as an advocate for mothering.

Mentors for mothers at home

But it is not only women who work or mothers who are trading business suits for jeans who need mentoring. Mothers who stay home for a season are also struggling to find older women who will invest in their lives. In an earlier era young girls grew up in the bosom of extended families with aunts, cousins, and grandmothers filling the role of mentors. They learned what they needed to know from women who naturally populated their lives. I spent my early years surrounded by women who fleshed out my identity: my Aunt Geneva, Aunt Ruby, Granny, Mother, Aunt Nancy, Aunt Stella, and Aunt Faye. Then when I married at twenty-two, I spent that first summer just hanging out at Granny's, canning peaches, ironing my husband's shirts, and cooking.

Mostly, I just hung out. A wife now, I went to my grandmother for companionship and instruction in housewifery. I still iron my husband's shirts as Granny instructed: collar first, shoulders, both sleeves, then the trunk. I am pleased she taught me how to do this simple task—her way. It's part of a small legacy from Granny that I've passed on to my daughters.

Sadly, few women today spend the first eighteen years of their lives in the company of an extended family. For most, grandmothers live across the country, and aunts and cousins are rarely seen except at weddings and funerals. Yet, young women need older women to teach them important life tasks: how to be an adult, how to nurture their children, how to love their husbands, how to nurture themselves.

A mentor is a friend for all seasons: marriage, motherhood, menopause. She helps us open and close key chapters in our lives.

Mentors teach us how to stay married

With an escalating divorce rate and a culture that condones adultery, we need all the help we can get for our marriages. Who better to help us fortify our marriages than someone who has had a satisfying and successful union herself?

When Don and I went through rough times during the girls' adolescence, I learned a lot from my friend Eleanor. Although my age, Eleanor has been successful in an area where I experienced failure. As I shared my occasional discouragement about my marriage, Eleanor not only gave me hope, but she imparted a vision for marriage based on her rock-solid, thirty-plus-year union with her husband, Frank, and on what she had learned growing up in an intact family. By sharing her feelings and perceptions, Eleanor would send me home ready to work harder on my marriage.

"I watched my mom and dad work things out," said Eleanor of her parents' long and satisfying marriage. "I remember seeing them dance together in the living room and just have fun." As Eleanor shared what her parents had taught her, I grew. I listened intently because I knew she loved Frank and was satisfied with their marriage.

Having been mentored by others in my marriage to Don, it is now my turn to mentor other young wives. I just got off the phone with a friend whose spouse is having an affair and has filed for divorce. I urged my friend to live a moral life and to use her energies to help her girls deal with their grief and pain. "The worst thing you can do," I said, "is become romantically involved right now. Look at your own issues, your responsibility for the marital failure, and take your pain and bitterness to God. Love and comfort your girls." I try to pass on to her what I have learned through Eleanor and others.

Mentors and mothering

Not only can mentors teach us about marriage, but they can also teach us how to become better mothers. After all, many of them were diapering babies and dealing with colic before we were born. What new mother hasn't yearned for some on-line instruction from a more seasoned mother?

When I was doing my doctoral research at three metropolitan hospitals, I often asked the new mothers if they would have help once they returned home with their babies. Most had mothers coming to help initiate them into the joys of motherhood, but some returned to empty homes with only a day or two of on-line help from their husbands. I felt compassion for these women because new motherhood is a time of high demand. Many of the mothers I interviewed felt uneasy at the thought of bathing their babies, and some viewed breast-feeding as a daunting experience, particularly if they were recovering from painful Cesareans.

Sue Huml, who has worked with La Leche League International for years, has been a mentor to many young moms. The mother of two college-age children, Sue says, "I have a home-based business, but when the phone rings, I drop everything to help a mom who's struggling to breast-feed her baby. I try to teach young mothers that their babies don't need a mansion or a lot of toys. Their babies need them." She adds that La Leche League is built on the premise that mentoring is essential for mothers.

One mother said, "Young moms today are confused about how to relate to new babies. We get such conflicting messages about what our babies need from us. And we are sometimes clueless in the area of discipline."

This is why the injunction in Titus 2:4 is compelling. Here, older women are enjoined to train the younger women to love their husbands and children, to be self-controlled, to be busy at home, to be kind, and to be cooperative with their husbands.

We who are older—and most of us are older to some young woman— are supposed to train young women, then, in several areas: marriage, child rearing, self-control, time management, and compassion. That will take much thought and no little time. As Jan Johnson says in *Virtue*, "As in any relationship, mentoring involves give and take, sharing, tackling goals together. It's a ministry of presence, empowering women with love and insight that is more caught than taught." She believes that mentors don't need to supply all the answers; instead they listen intently to the questions, "looking further down the road for us."[3]

Mentors as surrogate mothers

It is sometimes possible to find a mentor who can give us a measure of acceptance if we can't be friends with our mothers .

When Dee was a child, her mother left her with a succession of nannies while she pursued an active social life. So Dee grew up longing for a stable, surrogate mother, "someone who baked cookies and had a big lap to climb up in." Fortunately, in adulthood her mother-in-law became the mothering presence Dee longed for. This woman was able to meet her daughter-in-law's need for mothering and, in the process, help heal some old, deep wounds.

Even if we have close friendships with our mothers, we can still profit from in-depth, committed mentoring relationships with older women because our mothers can't teach us all we need to know about life, work, and relationships. Mentors can round out the female experience.

I encourage my daughters to have friendships with older women who have different personalities and life experiences than I. Rather than viewing this as competition, I understand that I have worked from home and lack the savvy and knowledge of the organization that many careerists have. So each daughter can profit from having a professional mentor who understands the corporate workplace.

The rewards of mentoring

What are the rewards of mentoring? Mentoring, particularly in midlife, prepares us for an emotionally rich old age.

Harvard psychoanalyst Erik Erikson states that the task of midlife (which begins between the ages of thirty-five and forty) is generativity. Erikson defines generativity as "guiding the next generation," "productivity," or "creativity."[4] He believes that if we nurture the younger generation, we are more likely to face old age with integrity. But if we fail in this task, we will not only experience stagnation in midlife but will face old age with crippling despair.[5]

Or, simply, as one of my English professors at Wheaton College, Clyde S. Kilby, said about his students when he was approaching eighty, "They keep me young."

Mentoring, then, is a necessary developmental task for the mentor and a gift to the protégé. When we women of a certain age give something back to the culture, we not only experience rich friendships, but we fill our lives with meaning and purpose. And this sense of meaning and purpose fortifies us for the end. As older women, we need to share our rich legacy of wisdom and experience with younger moms. For as we help a mother, we help her family. As families go, so goes society.

How to mentor

Okay. So some of you want to find mentors, and others of you want to become mentors. How to get together? In her article in *Virtue* Beth Sharpton encouraged both younger and older women to reach out to each other. "Invite a woman you'd like to know for coffee and extend invitations to upcoming events. Ask her to teach you a skill." I would add: ignore your fear of rejection and suggest that you two meet for lunch or dinner, attend a lecture, or go to an event together.

If you're the younger, ask the older woman questions about her life choices and how she reared her children or helped create a marriage. If you need advice for the workplace, find a mentor at the office or an expert in your field. Take her to lunch and learn from her. Ask if she would meet with you periodically to guide your career decisions. If you want to grow spiritually, find someone who can become a spiritual advisor to you. This was a common practice in an earlier era. In fact, Fenelon, the seventeenth century Archbishop of Cambrai, was the spiritual advisor for a young French woman in the court of Louis XIV, and he wrote wonderful letters to her which have been compiled into a devotional classic.

If you're the older, discover the areas of stress in the younger woman's life, and share your wisdom and practical help. Remember the words of

Beth Sharpton as you pass younger women throughout your day at the office, church, or mall. Younger women may wear the facade of independence, but inwardly "many struggle with inferiority, loneliness, fatigue, and self-doubt."

These are painful emotions that most of us have struggled with at some point in our lives. I can reach out. You can too. And as we do, we find that these younger women will enrich our lives in ways we can hardly imagine. We need their input as much as they need ours.

I have had the experience of mentoring several younger women, which has been richly rewarding. A picture of one of these mothers and her baby sits in a silver frame on my mantle. When the mother gave it to me, she said, "This is from Jonathan. He wants you to know he has had a mother at home for three years in part because of your influence." Whenever I see that picture, I smile.

Isn't that what life is all about? To pass the torch to younger families, to share what we're learning from our tragedies as well as our successes, to help strengthen America's families? The impact can last for generations to come.

Virginia Duran was born in migrant camps and grew up in neighborhoods that "reeked of petroleum, brine and rotting fish." At her birth a physician, a single woman named Virginia, had given the mother free medical care, and so the infant was named after her mother's benefactor.

The older Virginia provided food and clothing and a vision for her namesake, telling the younger girl that she too had been helped as a child. Having a benefactor—a mentor—helped young Virginia cope with her father's drunken brawls and her mother's eventual abandonment. Young Virginia eventually ended up in an orphanage with her siblings. Her mom's last letter read: "I'm going away. I don't know when I'll come back. Be a good girl and take care of the young ones."

Virginia eventually went to college and had a series of jobs after graduation. After eleven years she found herself in Baja, Mexico, caring for children abandoned in the migrant labor camps. Today, she cares for thirty-five children, knowing she does so because someone cared for her.

In fact, Virginia Duran is the seventh generation of Virginias. "All of them lived in the West, all of them were surrogate mothers for children who desperately needed loving, all of them were raised to pray for the children who would follow."[6]

Said the younger to the older

A final thought. Mentoring has a long history. In fact, one of the loveliest passages in all of literature is found in the Old Testament, and it describes a relationship between two women—one younger, the other, older. These women were not sisters, or mother and daughter, or simply friends. Although they were related by marriage, they were bound together by something deeper than mere blood ties. The younger woman felt deep love and compassion for the older woman in her life. Listen to these famous words I have entitled, "Said the Younger to the Older."

> Entreat me not to leave you
> or to return from following you;
> for where you go I will go,
> and where you lodge I will lodge;
> your people shall be my people,
> and your God my God.[7]

These words, often read at weddings to fuel the fire of marital love, are, of course, the words of Ruth to her unhappy mother-in-law, Naomi. Embittered by the loss of her husband and two sons, Naomi faced a poverty-stricken and uncertain future. "Leave me," she told her two daughters-in-law. One did. But not Ruth. Ruth stayed and became the consummate picture of loyalty, commitment, and obedience in a relationship with an older woman she loved dearly. As the story unfolds, we see that God honored Ruth's devotion. Because of Naomi, Ruth met Boaz, an older, wealthy man who became her husband. Because of Ruth, Naomi had grandchildren, economic provision, status, and the position as the Wise Woman at the city gates.

What richer portrait of the mentoring relationship could there be?

• • •

Kristie's Story

Having support as a mother at home has had a profound effect on my life, forever changing me as a woman and mother. Home became a place of healing, and the support of an older, caring woman helped shape the mother I am today. Without that loving touch, I am sure I would never have had the courage to face the cavernous void inside of me left by an emotionally impoverished childhood.

I had managed to keep those feelings at bay for many years by building a successful career. I never stepped off the fast track long enough even to realize my hidden pain. It wasn't until my son was born and my husband and I made the decision for me to stay at home that I finally confronted my past.

The first year was the hardest. I had become so task-oriented as an elementary school teacher that it was difficult to transition from career to home. It was difficult to come to closure on any activity with a newborn who altered his schedule weekly and housework that reappeared daily. I often felt tired and frazzled. It was also hard to feel validated at home when society didn't recognize the significance of my job as a mother. I found myself defensive and angry. When people asked what I did for a living, I usually told them I was a "procreation specialist" and laughed at their blank stares.

After a year I finally found a small band of mothers in my neighborhood who provided the support I needed during my son's infancy. Soon I was planning play group activities and starting a baby-sitting co-op for my new friends. The anger melted as I became more comfortable as a mother.

Two years after coming home to be with my son, our daughter was born. This rounded out our family to four and mysteriously shrunk the size of our home like an old wool sweater. Soon we were house hunting in a quiet suburb. As our family settled into our new surroundings, I was shocked to find that my new neighborhood resembled a desert after seven o'clock in the morning. I kept wondering where all the mothers had gone and who was taking care of the kids. I knew I couldn't be the only mother at home.

After several months of feeling lonely and grieving the loss of my friends, I decided to take action. I responded to an ad in the newspaper for a mothers' coffee. It was a support group for mothers at home. The speaker was an older woman who had walked before me as a mother. I listened intently as she spoke lovingly of her years at home with her children and related her vision for mothers at home. I went up to her afterwards and shared my story. Ann was warm and relational. I felt an immediate kinship with her. I signed up to lead a support group in my area, and she promised to direct me through the process.

I led that group for a year and a half. During that time, this woman acted as a mentor and also became a friend. She not only taught me how to lead a group but also to write articles, prepare for radio and television appearances, and lead training seminars for other leaders. She constantly built me up, taught me to dream big, and gave me opportunities to stretch myself.

But more important than managerial skills, this mentor grew me as a mother. As I shared with her my deepest secrets, she listened to my heart and always encouraged me through the difficult times. She was a rock, stable and secure. She was always there, full of support and wisdom, helping me shape my vision as a mother, a molder of human beings. Her loving touch has left an indelible mark not only on my life, but on the lives of my husband and children as well.

Just recently a friend who has had an abusive past called and said, "Kristie, I want to tell you that you've taught me about intimacy.

As you've been my friend, I've learned from you how to get close to my husband and children."

"Really?" I said. Then I remembered. "I didn't teach you about intimacy, but my mentor did. She taught me and I passed it on to you."

And that's the beauty of mentoring.

A former teacher of the gifted and talented, Kristie Tamillow has spent years homeschooling her children. Now she is giving concerts and occasionally defending motherhood on national TV. She and her husband, Mike, and their children, Matt and Meggie, live in Centerville, Virginia.

15

• • •

My Mentor/Myself

You never know when someone may catch a dream from you.
Helen Lowrie Marshall

I have realized only recently how fortunate I was in having a neighbor, an aunt by marriage, a minister's wife, and an employer—women who were not directly tied to me by biology—to enter my life, stay for a while, and leave me changed forever.

The first woman who reached out to me was a neighbor. I was thirteen years old, and my mother was battling her own inner demons. Martha lived next door to us in the Wachovia Apartments in Winston-Salem, North Carolina. Not only did Martha befriend me, but, aware of my mother's troubles, she often invited me for dinner or took me to church with her family. She was the first person who expressed interest in my spiritual development and invited me to help her with her child evangelism classes. Martha had an intimate relationship with God and shared her life experiences with me. When her alcoholic husband disappeared, leaving her and her daughter with little money, groceries magically appeared at her door, and money to pay the rent seemed to float in from anonymous benefactors. "See what God has done for us," said this ebullient midlife woman to a skeptical teenager. Over time her infectious faith overcame my resistance.

And largely because of Martha, and God's use of Martha, I am a woman of faith today.

It was Martha who introduced me to the poetry of Edna St. Vincent Millay, took me to tea at the elegant old Robert E. Lee Hotel with her young daughter, Celeste, when she had only ten dollars in her purse ("Never forget hyacinths for the soul," she said), and encouraged me to go to a midwestern, Christian college. She, a former secretary, even typed my application to Wheaton and introduced me to a Wheaton College cheerleader.

Also at this time Gladys, my minister's wife, took an interest in me. A mother of five, Gladys was a patrician southern woman. After the birth of each child, she listened to classical music as she nursed her babies. With her soft voice and lovely smile, Gladys taught me that motherhood is a richly rewarding experience. I remember when she called me just hours after the birth of her fifth child to share her joy. "I see stars on my ceiling," she gushed. I, a high school senior at the time, was jaundiced by this outpouring of mother love. But a part of me listened and responded to this woman who, unlike my own mother, felt that children were a gift to be enjoyed.

And when Gladys would drive me home after an evening of baking cookies and talking, she and I would sit in her station wagon and she would intone sweetly fervent prayers. Something inside felt warmed, cared for.

When I was a senior in high school, Gladys, an ace seamstress, made me a lovely lavender linen dress with a reversible jacket lined in silk for Easter. How this minister's wife with five children found the time and inclination to do that for a teenager, I'll never know. But I was deeply moved.

In addition to Martha and Gladys, Stella Owen entered my life when I was in elementary school. She later married my bachelor uncle, Blake.

What did Stella, a petite brunette who worked as an executive secretary for two North Carolina congressmen, give me? She introduced me to one of the healthiest families I have ever known—her own. In Stella's family all of the twelve children related to each other lovingly. Her parents, an engaging couple I met the summer I turned twelve, instilled high self-esteem and a strong sense of family in each child.

Stella, a nurturing woman, frequently invited me to the gracious home she shared with Uncle Blake, and together they introduced me to the bigger, broader world of Washington, D.C. After living in a duplex apartment with my mother—we paid fifteen dollars a month in rent—it was a mind-expanding experience to tour our nation's capitol.

In addition, she and my uncle often did the parental things in my life. When I was a frightened freshman about to enter Wheaton, Stella paid for my first plane trip and took me there and helped me furnish my room. Each summer she and Blake bought me lovely clothes to take to college. Later they were the only members of my family to attend my college graduation or to contribute to my wedding expenses.

In addition to these three nurturing women, during my college years I met another woman who has been a mentor and a continuing presence throughout my adult life—Marty Clansky.

Marty hired me as her cleaning girl for ninety cents an hour when I was a callow, untutored eighteen-year-old. At the time, ours was a business arrangement; neither of us had any idea that a significant and lasting friendship would result. She was a young mother in her early thirties, and I was a college freshman. She needed help with her housework and child care; I needed money for college expenses.

I wasn't particularly excited about becoming a cleaning lady within a few days of arriving at college. After all, my mother had never made me work but had raised me to become a rich man's wife. Nonetheless, I agreed to meet Marty and soon was trudging the several blocks to her rambling house on Forest Avenue, kicking leaves as I went. As I walked, I talked to myself. It was true that I needed to earn money. I had turned down a full scholarship at Duke University to attend Wheaton. The college had promised no financial help, and I was anxious about how I would pay my bills. But clean someone's toilets?

Marty, an attractive thirty-four-year-old with short, brown hair, greeted me at the door and smiled as she invited me into her sunny living room. Green wingbacks flanked the fireplace, and green and blue hues were picked up in the furniture around the room. Coming from rented, dingy apartments, I knew I was definitely entering another social strata.

I liked Marty instantly and was even amused by silent, blond Bill, her three-year-old who peeked at me from behind his mother. We agreed that I would start to work the next day. In my immaturity I had no idea that what Marty would teach me would have any ultimate value. I could not foresee that just as Marty taught her ten-year-old daughter to bake cookies, bread, and cakes, I too would follow her example and teach my daughters the basics of cooking when they were nine and ten. As a result, today Holly makes exquisite meals for her friends from the *Silver Palate* cookbook, and Kristen is comfortable feeding twenty.

Years earlier, when the girls were very young, I began to read aloud nightly from *Mother Goose,* holding each close to me just as I had seen Marty hold Bill close to her as she read stories from children's classics.

And over lunches consisting of homemade whole wheat bread, roast beef, and fresh fruit, I developed a friendship with this woman. Marty had never completed college, but she possessed an intelligent, inquiring mind. She quizzed me about the books I was reading as a lit major, and in time she was reading along with me in our two-member literary club.

Throughout my years at Wheaton the Clansky family became increasingly important to me. Once Marty and Roy hosted a party for ten of my friends, acting as butler and chef. While my friends were duly impressed that the president of a Chicago steel forgings company and his wife were willing to host a group of college students, I was touched. I could not recall a single birthday party growing up.

The summer after my junior year the Clanskys invited me to live with them. I spent several weeks in the north woods of Wisconsin helping Marty around the house. Once she entertained the president of Wheaton, Dr. V. Raymond Edmond, who was vacationing nearby, and I was able to sit in the presence of this deeply spiritual man who spoke in chapel of Wheaton students as "brave sons and daughters true." Our days at the lake were filled with reading, walking, and swimming and water-skiing in frigid water. Such simple experiences. But I had never had a family that took summer vacations together. So this was especially meaningful for me.

The Clanskys' most significant act of kindness occurred during my senior year at a time when I felt particularly vulnerable. I had taken David, my fiancé, home to spend Christmas with my mother, who was living alone and working as a telephone operator at the Baptist Hospital in Winston-Salem. I had hoped, had prayed, that mother would be stable during the holidays. I had explained to David that she had significant personality problems but knew he had never seen anything like my mother at her chaotic worst.

I hoped in vain. When Christmas Day arrived, Mother flew into a rage, accusing us of sexual misconduct. I was deeply humiliated by her false allegations and David watched helplessly. He was due to fly home to Buffalo that afternoon, but the streets were icy, and no taxi would risk coming to take him to the airport. I remember going next door to the young medical resident, a stranger, to ask if he would drive David to the airport. Graciously, he agreed.

Days later I fled back to Wheaton, devastated and afraid David would reconsider marrying me. I had borrowed twelve dollars from Granddaddy to help pay for train fare and found myself in the Chicago train station with only two dollars and twenty-five cents left—a quarter to call Marty and Roy and two dollars for a ticket on the commuter train to Wheaton. Fortunately, the Clanskys took me in. After all, the campus was closed and I couldn't get into my dorm. The next day as I was vacuuming, Roy walked up to me and extended a twenty dollar bill. "Here," he said cheerfully, "this must be yours. I think you dropped it while you were cleaning."

Thirty years later I still feel deeply touched when I remember Roy's gift. He protected my self-esteem while showing more concern for my welfare than my own immediate family.

Over the years Marty has continued to be a comforting, wise presence in my life. We have visited each other on occasion, and both Holly and Kris have flown to California to spend time with Marty and Roy. I sometimes overhear Kris, who never had a grandfather, tell friends that Marty and Roy are her adopted grandparents. And I? I have become an older friend to two of Marty's children.

Fast forward to November 1993. Marty and I are sitting in the elegant tea room of a local hotel. Marty and Roy have come to the Washington area for their annual visit with their son's family, and she has driven down from

Bethesda, Maryland, to spend some time with me today. The previous Sunday when Marty and Roy came for dinner, Don was there, along with Holly and Kristen and their boyfriends. We had a lovely, rich day together. But that was family time; today is woman time. For a few, all too brief, hours I will be in the company of a woman who continues to impact my thinking and my life.

When we finally settle into a comfy chair and sofa and the waitress brings our plate of huge strawberries slathered with cream, another plate loaded with scrumptious tea cakes, and two companion pots of English Breakfast tea, we begin to talk in earnest. She, now sixty-nine, updates me on her family—Bill, Pam, Fred, Grandma Clansky, and Ken and Gina and their three children. I talk about Don's work situation and the girls' romances.

As we confide in each other, I note that Marty looks tired (probably after being with small grandchildren for ten straight days) and that she looks older than she did on Sunday. We discuss our estrogen regimen. I feel comforted that as I move into the uncharted territory of postmenopause, Marty has traveled before me. Her midlife passage was handled with verve, optimism, and integrity. Her adult children are leading busy, productive lives and yet stay close to Marty and Roy. I hope Holly and Kristen will do the same. Marty coaches me on letting go, on the fruits of marriage in young old age, on being an active, healthy woman. She tells me what it feels like to be a grandmother. I can see that she is moving deeper into a companionate marriage and that she speaks of Roy, her seventy-two, jovial husband, with even greater warmth than I remember in her thirties. Through Marty I see that marriage can grow richer in "young old age."

Too quickly our time together ends. Roy returns from his solo shopping excursion, having purchased a book on bankruptcy in the nineties, and joins us for tea. Later he asks wryly, "Why is it that he who comes late gets to pay the bill?" We laugh, knowing that Roy is pleased to be a part of the experience.

When it is time to leave, Marty says to me, "Why don't you and Don come out to California after you finish your book. I'd like to have you on my turf. Then we can really talk." I promise to come and we say our good-byes—two silver-haired women, bound together by an invisible cord of love and friendship for thirty-four years.

Mentoring—extending a hand

I remember talking to a Catholic priest once who said that throughout his life, at difficult or important times, someone had come along and extended a hand. He took the hand and walked with that person for a time, feeling comforted, stretched as a person, growing deeper in his faith in God.

I love that image of the outstretched hand. Each of us on occasion needs someone to come along and extend a hand. We, on the other hand, need to take the hand and walk together for a time.

I have been fortunate during my lifetime to have had several women invest their time—themselves—in me. Whether I recruited them or they reached out to me is a moot point. In truth, we reached out to each other: I, a needy young girl, they, intelligent and compassionate women of deep religious faith. Because they came, my whole life has been healthier, richer, deeper. I realize, of course, who sent these helpful people to a southern girl who often felt lonely and vulnerable growing up. And because of these "witnesses" and all they've meant to me, I have tried to reach out to other women. To increase their resiliency. To extend a hand.

◆　◆　◆

She Gave the Softest Hugs

It's a cool morning in May, and as I clean up the kitchen, I'm looking forward to working in the garden and yard. Taking off my apron, I fondly remember my mother-in-law, Phyllis, who gave me this purple and green apron because it no longer fit her.

Ever since Phyllis passed away, the apron has taken on a special meaning and brings back memories. If one image comes to mind, it's of Phyllis waiting for us to arrive from out of town Wearing a housecoat, slippers, and a long apron hanging from her shoulders to her knees, she would invite us into her warm kitchen. I never thought of her as being an "old fatty" as she often referred to herself with self-deprecating humor. Rather, she exemplified all the traits of the quintessential grandma. Phyllis was caring and giving, and she had an aura of peaceful serenity. My younger daughter summed it up well when she once said, "Grandma gives the softest hugs!" Even in her later years, I could still see the beauty in her strong Greek features of wavy black hair, the smoothest creamy skin, and big brown eyes.

Her kitchen always looked the same: dinner warming on the stove and cookies in tins cluttering the kitchen table. She was especially famous for her homemade koulourakia (butter twist cookies, which my kids called "twisty" cookies) and the best chocolate chip cookies I've ever eaten—I've never been able to duplicate them. Quite modest in her accomplishments, she'd say she couldn't cook gourmet meals. In wearing her apron today, I can only hope her talent rubs off on me.

I can still hear her voice, "Hi, Paaaam!" And we'd hug and kiss. We'd sit at the kitchen table, she and I, and we'd talk about the latest family news. She'd reach out and tap me on the arm to make a point, her affectionate way of emphasizing something. Her interests revolved around her family, and she was perfectly content in making them the focus of her life.

On the surface, one would think we didn't have a lot in common. I'm involved in a wide variety of activities and spend time away from home almost every day. Phyllis, on the other hand, preferred to stay close to home. But the warmth of home and family life was our common bond. In addition to that, we both loved to have a good laugh, and we both liked the color purple—we often would exchange purple items for gifts.

Even though, at times, we were separated by several states and neither one of us liked to pay for long distance telephone calls, we managed to keep in touch by writing letters to each other.

She always addressed them just to me. "I went to town today to pay our electric and water bills, stopped by Stone and Thomas to pay on the layaway. We had three inches of snow and it's been colder than usual" were typical lines from her letters. They came often enough that I began to expect them, and I could almost predict their arrival.

Early on in my marriage, Phyllis said I could call her Mom. Having married so young (at twenty-one) and having a loving and close relationship with my own mother, I couldn't imagine calling her "Mom" when she invited me to do so. But I was quick to tell my new mother-in-law that it didn't mean I loved her any less. She never mentioned it again, and I think I proved to her over the fifteen years I knew her how genuine my feelings were. We truly got along quite well and got to be good pen pals. I'd write newsy letters filled with details of all our activities. Phyllis would write back, telling me how much she loved reading my letters or how she laughed as she read about the antics of her grandchildren.

Christmas was her favorite holiday, and she loved to bake, decorate, and shop for presents for everyone she knew. And if we weren't going to be able to get together for the Easter holiday, we'd receive a special package through the mail. It would be filled with chocolate candy and several loaves of her special homemade Easter bread. It was so good, the kids and I wouldn't bother using a knife or butter; we'd just rip right into it. I'm sure Phyllis would have laughed if she had seen us.

Phyllis never finished high school but kept the family budget perfectly balanced and put three kids through college on a steelworker's paycheck. She instilled in her children tremendous values, as well as a deep respect for themselves and others.

It was May 1990 when Andy's mom and dad decided to visit. Mother's Day that year was the same weekend as our daughter Samantha's ninth birthday. Andy, Samantha, and her sister

Alexandra went shopping and bought pretty lavender and green scented candles and soaps and baskets, a few things they knew Grandma would like.

As usual, Phyllis and Andrew were scheduled to arrive from West Virginia around lunch time on Friday. Instead of a knock at the door announcing their arrival, the phone rang, and a voice said "Mrs. Goresh? I'm calling from the Hagerstown Hospital in Maryland. Your father-in-law is fine, but your mother-in-law became ill on the trip and died of a heart attack."

Hours later, I sat alone in the living room. What could I say? What could I do?

Andy had driven to Hagerstown to meet his father. When Andy and his dad returned, words stuck in my throat and tears spilled from my eyes to see Andrew walk in alone. Andrew, with red-rimmed eyes, hugged me and said, "Phyllis was so happy that morning. She was looking forward to celebrating Samantha's birthday, and you know, she just loved all those letters you wrote. They meant so much to her."

When I talked with Phyllis's sister, Mary, about funeral arrangements, Mary mentioned that Phyllis had always loved the color pink. "Phyllis should be laid to rest in a pink dress," she added. How about that. All those years she'd let me think her favorite color was purple so we would have something in common.

As I passed her casket, I picked up a pink flower, paused, and thought, "No, Phyllis and I shared purple." I put the pink flower down and reached instead for a lovely lavender iris and gave it to her.

Pam Goresh is editor-in-chief of Welcome Home, *the monthly magazine produced by Mothers at Home in northern Virginia. She has been a mother at home for twelve years and lives in Ellicott City, Maryland, with her husband, Andy, and daughters Samantha, twelve, and Alexandra, nine.*

16

. . .

The Legacy

When I stopped seeing my mother with the eyes of a child,

I saw a woman who helped me give birth to myself.

Nancy Friday, writer

s I leave my hundred-year-old farmhouse in northern Virginia for Amish country, I soon become mired in heavy traffic—the joy of living in metropolitan Washington, D.C. where traffic snarls, day or night, are as predictable as the seasonal changes. Finally we move forward, and I am free. West of Baltimore, I see rolling hills and farms. My body begins to relax. Two hours later I reach my destination: Lancaster, Pennsylvania.

Why have I come to Amish country during the last pressure-packed days of writing this book? I have come to interview three generations of women—Mary, Sydney, and Kelly—all descendants of Harvey and Martha Owen.

Harvey, a school teacher, married his petite, hundred-pound student Martha when she was sixteen. She would later become a local "mother-in-law of the year." Together they had twelve children and seventy-three years of a happy, satisfying marriage. When their children were growing up, Harvey polished twelve pairs of shoes nightly and tutored his and the neighbor's children. Martha shared her washing machine with nearby extended family and happily fed all of her children's myriad friends when the family ate their three meals together. And each evening the family read the Bible together.

Of the twelve children, ten are alive today and six are in their eighties. What each remembers most about his or her childhood is growing up feeling like the best-loved child. All twelve of them.

The Owen family has long fascinated me since I met Harvey and Martha when I was twelve. My aunt Stella, an Owen herself, and Uncle Blake had taken me to Mt. Nebo, Pennsylvania, to visit them. As I tramped around the farm with the small white house, even then I understood that this couple and their family possessed something I hungered for and did not always find in my immediate family. I watched them affirm, support, and care for each other in real and practical ways. They helped each other through the crises of life: the illnesses and deaths, mostly of in-laws.

Even now, the descendants of Harvey and Martha meet yearly for Christmas dinner. About a hundred and thirty of them assemble from the four corners of the U.S. to celebrate Christmas in a school cafeteria in tiny Mt. Nebo, little more than a crossroads and a filling station.

When Harvey and Martha were still alive, the clan would gather again for a summer corn roasting at the family farm. Dozens of grandchildren ran mad, scrambling to be the first to jump into the swimming pool.

As I drive down farm-lined roads to Sydney's sprawling ranch-style house, I wonder how this interview will go. Mary's husband, Frank, a retired chef who believed in putting family first, was buried last Tuesday. He was ninety. How, I wonder, will the three women handle their grief?

Soon Mary, Kelly, and I are sitting in Sydney's comfy living room in front of a welcoming fire. Books line the walls—books of poetry that Sydney, a seventh grade teacher, has collected. Kelly, Sydney's thirty-year-old daughter, and Mary, her attractive eighty-eight-year-old mother, sit facing each other. They are soon talking animatedly.

Kelly, an addictions counselor who works with adolescents, begins. "The women in my family are strong and confident," she says. "We share a firm belief in family."

Although Kelly's parents divorced when she was a vulnerable thirteen-year-old, Kelly's mother and grandparents provided the stability she needed. "My grandparents had open arms. Always. I could go to them with anything without ever feeling judged. Even now I can tell Gram anything." She smiles at the matriarch of the clan. "And Gram's fun! Just the other night we were both in Mom's kitchen at three o'clock, discussing my date of that night."

Mary sits quietly as Kelly speaks words of love and admiration. Nearing her ninth decade, Mary is still a pretty woman with blue, blue eyes and gray hair that frames her face. Although she has just buried her husband of sixty-eight years, she is surprisingly serene. "My doctor tells me I'm lucky," she says. "Some children would want a parent my age to go to a nursing home, but Sydney wants me to live with her. In fact, both Frank and I had planned to move here before he died."

Kelly and Mary tell me how much they miss Frank. They reminisce. When Frank heard that Kelly was born, he was so excited that he ran ten blocks to the hospital, forgetting his car. A doting grandfather, he would push his old push mower with one hand while cradling Kelly in his other arm. Mary says Kelly was a mainstay in her life during the days of his illness and death. The bond between Mary and her granddaughter is almost tangible as we three sit in the quiet room.

As we wait for Sydney to return from her evening graduate class, I question Mary, "What was your relationship with your mother like?"

"We were very, very close," said Mary. "I adored my mother. I still marvel at how she took care of all of us and yet had time to talk to each of us as well. She was so patient and kind. And she never had an enemy. She was not a strict person, but we understood what we could and couldn't do. Everyone felt they were special to her, and yet she had no favorites. But when one of us got sick, the sick one received extra care. I remember once going to visit my parents alone. That night my mother came to my room after I had gone to bed just to see if I was warm or if I needed anything. I was over fifty at the time!"

At that moment, Sydney, a perky fifty-three-year-old, sails into the room and introduces herself. A woman without a hint of gray in her brown hair, Sydney quickly enters into the conversation.

"Tell me about your relationship with your mother," I ask.

"My mother," says Sydney, looking at Mary, "is sensitive, caring, and loyal. She is also a beautiful woman. There were five of us children, and we had a carefree childhood. One of my best memories is of playing store with the boxes Mother saved from her shopping excursions. We were allowed to create anything; Mother was not concerned about the mess.

"Mother always listened to me, but she was strict. She had expectations that I would become a loyal, honest human being. And she, who continues to learn new things at eighty-eight, encouraged me never to stop learning.

"But the best thing my mother gave me was her unconditional love. No matter what happened, her love was there. It continues to be there. What does that feel like? It feels warm, secure, happy. It gives me confidence. I can take risks. I can make decisions," says Sydney who values her hard-won independence as a single woman.

Sydney says her parents were supportive when they knew her marriage was over. "I had been an at-home mother," says Sydney, "so when I went back to school, my mother drove thirty miles each way every day to pick up Chad, my five-year-old, after kindergarten. My parents gave me bags of groceries, called to see if I needed anything, and encouraged me to finish my bachelor's degree so I could take care of my children." Sydney pauses. "I remember the first Christmas after my divorce. I couldn't make any decisions then, even simple ones. I was exhausted. My parents told me to lie down, to take a break. They took care of my children and never gave up on me—never. They put all their love behind me, and I managed to survive that devastating time because of them. They always made me believe I could do anything I needed to do."

Both Sydney and Kelly agree that their legacy of emotional security is a rarity in modern America. Sydney speaks of some of her students whom she feels have no real connection to anyone. She describes them as "emotionally abandoned kids who are astonished to hear me say, 'I like you. You're worthwhile.'" Kelly adds that many adolescents in America no longer understand the language of love. "It's like a foreign language to them," she says.

"It's so different with us." Sydney continues looking at her daughter, then her mother. "We share this legacy of inner security. If Mother and I were separated to the farthest points of the earth, we have a bond that would never break. Kelly and I are the same."

Kelly speaks of the teenagers she has worked with in the past ten years as a substance abuse counselor. Both Caucasian and African-American, these are the children of mothers who were victims of sexual abuse or parental loss. Kelly still keeps in touch with two of the boys, now eleven and thirteen, whose mother was a former client. Both have spent weeks several summers at Sydney's home.

Kelly employs her belief in unconditional love in her work. She says, "I never give up on my kids. Never. The kids want me to give up on them just like their parents have, and they test me. But I'm firm, and I teach the kids discipline to help turn them around. I see a lot of emptiness in the kids I work with. The majority have full-blown addictions and are from troubled families, so they're not getting the love and support they need. One of my clients said recently, 'Why not get high. Nobody cares. Nobody talks to me.' He's a ninth grader and he already feels like this."

Kelly helps her clients take responsibility for themselves, no matter what life has dealt them. "I try to plant a seed of hope—something my clients can look back to in the years ahead," she says. She talks to the two boys who come to visit about college. The boys recently paid Kelly their highest compliment, telling her that if they ever had a stepmother, they would want it to be her.

Sydney, like her daughter Kelly, feels she can make a difference in society. Sydney encourages her students to succeed and tells them she cares about them. "Teachers have an enormous opportunity to make a difference in kids' lives," Sydney says. "Unfortunately, we do a lot of labeling and don't always allow kids to get out of a box. That disturbs me."

I come back to the subject of divorce, knowing that even amid such strong family ties this had to be a wrenching experience for Sydney and her children. Kelly admits the divorce was necessary but painful.

"I admire my mom for what she did in keeping our family together," Kelly says. "I always respected her. That doesn't mean I always listened to her. Once when I was a senior in high school, I went out with friends and drank too much. Mom was upset, but she didn't scream. The next morning we sat down and talked, and that was enough. It didn't happen again. I was scared, but I was impressed with the way my mom handled me. I respected what she said—I still do."

"We've had our conflicts," says Sydney. "But one of us has always picked up the phone to call and say 'I'm sorry; we need to talk.' Or one of us will write a long letter saying, 'Life is too short; we need to work it out.'" She adds, "A sense of humor always helps."

Kelly agrees. "Sometimes I get angry and call Mom a jerk." She laughs. "I always know we'll come back and work it out. There's always something to come back to."

Mary listens and says she has never been afraid to apologize, whether she was wrong or not. She admits she could have held a grudge against a close relative "forever," but she felt bad about it and wanted to make things right.

Mary acknowledges that her life has had painful moments, but she looks back without regrets. "I've made my share of mistakes," she says. "I may have been too strict with the children, but I'm grateful I've had the patience to endure the ups and downs of life. I'm an optimist. I never look at the dark side of anything. Frank, whose mother died when he was ten and whose father was harsh, saw the dark side of everything."

Sydney agrees and adds, "My father would never have had ninety years without Mother; he would have given up. But Mother could get him to go out for an evening, even when he didn't want to. He always enjoyed himself once he was out of the house."

As we talk, I am impressed by Mary's view of aging. "I never think about my age. My doctor tells me my only problem is that I don't know how old I am," laughs Mary, who has erect posture and walks without a cane. She admits she has trouble with her heart and gets tired early in the day, but she has plans for her future and hopes to live past ninety. She knows Frank would want her to enjoy every day she has left.

"I'm not afraid of death," says Mary, "but I don't want to die just now. I'm like the teacher who said years ago, 'I want to go to heaven, but not today.'"

"I want to go back to my watercolors, or maybe write a novel," says this woman who compiled her family's genealogies in her eighties and in the process collected photographs and little anecdotes for two hundred members of her father's family. Mary tells me she has been in every state in the union except three and is eager to travel again. She and Kelly plan to visit the Wisconsin Dells in the near future. "I love this country, and I want to see every corner of it," Mary remarks.

Sydney shares her mother's love of life and feels that her mother is ageless. Sydney, a vibrant, alive woman, admits that she never thinks about aging. In a culture that emphasizes youth and encourages midlife women to try to turn back the clock, Sydney says, "I look at mother and I never see her stressed about growing older. That has certainly helped me. I don't wish I were a different age. Like my mother, I am concerned, not about aging, but about living my life."

At this point, I ask Sydney how her mother's love differed from her father's. Admitting that as a child she went to both parents for comfort, Sydney said she felt each parent gave her something unique. "My father thought I was nearly perfect, and that was a wonderful gift. But mother, as a woman, knew me and knew the pitfalls that lay ahead. She seemed to know intuitively how to guide me. Once when I was going out on a date, she watched me apply my makeup and gently said, 'There's just one thing you need to be beautiful. A smile.' I needed to hear that. Dad would have said, 'Of course you're beautiful.' Although I had a strong emotional bond with both parents, there's something about motherhood that's unique and almost beyond words."

As our evening draws to a close, the women recount an event that illustrates the invisible, almost telepathic bond they share across three generations. Days after Frank's funeral where Sydney and her daughter read aloud their tribute to a man they both loved, Mary and Sydney were driving home during an afternoon thunderstorm. Afterwards, they looked up and saw a rainbow shimmering in the sky.

"That's for Dad," said Sydney. Later when they got home and walked in the door, Mary asked Kelly, "Did you see it?" never mentioning what "it" was.

"I saw it," said Kelly, nodding, her eyes misting. "I saw the rainbow."

As I left Sydney's house that night, the sky was clear and the earth was frozen with the chill of winter. I headed for my motel, aware that I had just witnessed something unusual—three generations of women who talked easily and openly about their love and respect for each other. Because of their three-stranded cord of love, each can face the future, confident that no matter what life brings, she is not alone. She is—and will be—in the company of two other women she holds dear. And the blessings across the generations roll on.

Epilogue

S ince the publication of this book, I am hearing from women who tell me of their life-giving relationships with their mothers, daughters, and friends. But I am also hearing from those for whom these powerful bonds are missing. As I listen to their stories, whether on talk radio or in a whispered aside at a conference, I sense their raw, naked yearning for healing and restoration.

I will not soon forget one midthirties mother of five who called the radio station in Seattle where I was a guest. She had defied her mother by marrying a man her mother disliked, so her mother refuses to speak to her. Apparently this has gone on for years. "We live in the same neighborhood, but if I go to the grocery store and my mother comes in, she leaves as soon as she sees me," the woman said. Then, losing her composure, she wailed, "Why does she hate me so?"

Sometimes I feel hard-pressed to give an answer in the face of such deep human anguish. I know that no therapist, no matter how skilled or caring, can "fix" a hole in the soul or bring reluctant, warring family members together. Psychotherapy can only go so far.

So where do we go with our yearning and our painful relationships? We go to God, trusting that He will orchestrate the healing in ourselves and others that we desire.

Even as I write, God is healing my relationship with my sister, and our relationship with our mother. Let me share the events of a recent day with you.

જી

I am sitting in my mother's private room at Duke University Hospital while she sleeps. Her thinning white hair frames her tired and pinched face. Looking at her, I feel inwardly fragile. At seventy-four, Mother is in grave danger. The soft-spoken chief resident in internal medicine has just explained to me and my husband that Mother has numerous blood clots in her legs and possibly one in her lungs. "She could throw a clot at any time and die of pulmonary embolism," she says.

Don and I have driven to Durham, North Carolina, today to talk to Mother about the invasive procedures the doctors wish to do. Because she is resisting treatment, the doctors have turned to us to secure consent. The seriousness of her condition presses in on me. Feeling overwhelmed, I call my sister, Sandy. She was the daughter-on-call before Mother was transferred to Duke. Now it's my turn.

"Sandy," I weep as the doctors and nurses stream by, "Mother may die soon."

Sandy listens, then responds soothingly. "God is with Mother in this. And He is also healing our relationship with her and with each other."

We talk about the ways we see God at work: His provision of a caring Christian doctor during the stint at the small town hospital and the new spirit of cooperation between us as we work with the doctors and the manager of the nursing home where mother will go once she leaves Duke. Sandy tells me about her recent visit with Mother when Mother was warm and kind. Sandy, who came expecting hostility and rejection, sobbed in the parking lot after that visit, telling her husband, Ron, "If she had only been like this over the years, my whole life would have been different."

Both of us have struggled with our relationship with Mother. Forever. Both of us had our emotional bond to her broken in our early years. And while we have experienced a measure of healing in midlife, God is doing an even deeper work now.

I, the psychologist, hang up the phone, profoundly comforted by my wise and empathetic sister. When I return to Mother's room, I find her talking cheerfully to Don. He has always been able to communicate with her better than I. There's no intensity in their relationship. As I brush her hair, give her a manicure, and show her the gowns and robes I have brought, we talk about her treatment, the possibility of death, and her desires.

"Mother, are you afraid to die?" I ask.

"Brenda, there are things worse than death," she replies.

We speak about her life, the death of my father when she was twenty-two, her faith. I ask if she knows the Lord, and she responds that He has been her friend for years. "How do you think I could have endured the pain in my life without the Lord's help?" she asks.

I am consoled by her words. And as I do the little nurturing acts, years of pain continue to dissolve. Sandy is right. God is doing His alchemy. He continues to heal our relationship with our mother. He is doing what no psychologist could ever do as He arranges the circumstances of our lives and brings estranged family members together. The laser of his love penetrates the bruised and broken places in our hearts. I am confident that when this time of suffering passes I will look back and discover that God has created something beautiful in our lives.

Later Don and I leave Mother at the hospital to go out to eat. At the restaurant a black waitress asks why we have come to Durham. I start to cry and tell her my mother is seriously ill.

When we rise to leave, the waitress walks toward me and takes my hand. "What's her name?" she asks.

"Maureen."

"I'll pray for her," she whispers.

As we leave the restaurant, I sense the warm, comforting presence of the Lord. That simple event, as with the others of the day, bears His signature. And hope, rising like a phoenix from the ashes, fills my heart. God is on the move.

Notes

Chapter 1: The Necessary Company of Women

1. Carin Rubenstein, "A 1993 New Woman Survey," *New Woman* (October 1993): 78.
2. John Bowlby, *A Secure Base* (New York: Basic Books, 1988), 28.
3. Rubenstein, "New Woman Survey," 81.
4. Pat O'Connor, *Friendships Between Women* (New York: Guilford Press, 1992), 9-10.

Chapter 2: Mother: Our First Connection

1. Evelyn Thoman and Sue Browder, *Born Dancing* (New York: Harper and Row, 1987), 105.
2. Ibid.
3. Ibid., 112
4. Ibid., 113.
5. Ibid.

6. William Damon, *Social and Personality Development* (New York: W. W. Norton and Company, 1983), 87.

7. Ibid.

8. Donald W. Winnicott, "The Mother-Infant Experience of Mutuality," in *Parenthood: Its Psychology and Psychopathology,* ed. E. James Anthony and Therese Benedek (New York: Little, Brown and Company, 1970), 254-55.

9. Diane McClein Bengson, "To have and to hold," in *Discovering Motherhood,* ed. Heidi Brennan, Pamela Goresh, and Catherine Myers (Vienna, Va.: Mothers at Home Publishing, 1991), 27.

10. L. Alan Sroufe, "The Coherence of Individual Development," in *In the Beginning,* ed. Jay Belsky (New York: Columbia Press, 1982), 19.

11. Sigmund Freud, *Outline of Psychoanalysis,* 2d ed. (London: Hogarth Press, 1940), 188.

12. John Bowlby, *Attachment,* vol. 1 (New York: Basic Books, 1969), xi-xii.

13. Ibid.

14. Ross Parke and Barbara Tinsky, "Family Interaction in Infancy," in *Handbook of Infant Development,* ed. Joy D. Osofsky (New York: John Wiley and Sons, 1987), 589.

15. Ibid., 590.

16. Ibid.

17. John Bowlby, *Separation,* vol. 2 of *Attachment and Loss* (New York: Basic Books, 1973), 204-7.

18. Mary Ainsworth, "Patterns of Infant-Mother Attachments: Antecedents and Effects of Development," *Bulletin of New York Academy of Medicine,* 61 (November 1985): 776.

19. Sroufe, "Individual Development," 26-27.

20. Bowlby, *A Secure Base,* 124.

21. Ainsworth, "Patterns," 776.

22. Ibid.

23. Bowlby, *A Secure Base,* 128.

24. Ibid., 124.

25. Nancy Friday, *My Mother/Myself* (New York: Dell Publishers, 1977), vi.

26. Nancy Chodorow, *The Reproduction of Mothering* (Berkeley: University of California Press, 1978), 109.

27. Ruthellen Josselson, *Finding Herself: Pathways to Identity Development in Women* (San Francisco: Jossey-Bass, 1987), 171.

28. Ibid., 173.

29. Ibid.

30. Ibid.

31. Rubenstein, "New Woman Survey," 78-82.

32. Ibid., 82.

33. Linda Weber, *Mom, You're Incredible* (Colorado Springs, Colo.: Focus on the Family Publishers, 1994), 3-4.

Chapter 3: Mother Love

1. Margaret Ricks, "The Social Transmission of Parental Behavior: Attachment across Generations" in *Growing Points of Attachment Theory and Research*, ed. Inge Bretherton and Everett Waters, *Monographs of the Society for Research in Child Development*, vol. 50, nos. 1-2 (n.d.), 221.

2. Ibid., 213.

3. Ibid., 223.

4. M. D. S. Ainsworth, M. C. Blehar, E. Waters, and S. Wall, *Patterns of Attachment* (Hillsdale, N.J.: Erlbaum, 1978), 22.

Chapter 4: Mother Woe

1. Elaine McEwan, *My Mother, My Daughter* (Wheaton: Harold Shaw, 1992), 34.

2. Ibid., 35.

3. Victoria Secunda, *When You and Your Mother Can't Be Friends: Resolving the Most Complicated Relationship of Your Life* (New York: Dell Publishers, 1990), xv.

4. Ibid., 81.

5. Ibid., 84.

6. McEwan, *My Mother,* 117.

7. Secunda, *You and Your Mother,* 107.

8. Ibid.

9. Ibid., 114.

10. Ibid., 131.

11. Ibid., 139.

12. Bowlby, *Attachment,* xiii.

13. Ibid.

14. Anthony Storr, *The Art of Psychotherapy* (New York: Routledge, 1979), 99.

15. Adrienne Rich, *Of Woman Born: Motherhood as Experience and Institution* (New York: Norton and Co., 1976), 242-43.

16. Ibid., 243.

17. Secunda, *You and Your Mother,* xvi-xvii.

Chapter 5: Making Peace with Our Mothers

1. C. S. Lewis, ed., *George MacDonald: An Anthology* (London: Geoffrey Bles, 1970), 26.

2. McEwan, *My Mother,* 148.

3. John 1:5.

Chapter 6: Daughters: Our Mirror Images

1. Julie Firman and Dorothy Firman, *Daughters and Mothers: Healing the Relationship* (New York: Continuum, 1989), xiii.

2. Marianne Hirsch, "Mothers and Daughters" in *Ties that Bind,* ed. Jean O'Barr, Deborah Pope, and Mary Wyer (Chicago: University of Chicago Press, 1990), 183.

3. Eleanor E. Maccoby, *Social Development* (New York: Harcourt, Brace, Jovanovich, 1980), 221.

4. Ibid., 222.

5. Ibid., 223.

6. Anita C. Fellman, "Laura Ingalls Wilder and Rose Wilder Lane: The Politics of a Mother/Daughter Relationship," in *Ties that Bind*, ed. Jean O'Barr, Deborah Pope, and Mary Wyer (Chicago: University of Chicago Press, 1990), 232.

7. Ibid., 238.

8. Ibid., 237.

9. Juanita H. Williams, "The Emergence of Gender Differences," in *Social and Personality Development*, ed. William Damon (New York: W. W. Norton, 1983), 345.

10. William R. Mattox, Jr., "A Lesson for Allison," *Wall Street Journal*, 28 April 1994.

11. Edith Neisser, *Mothers and Daughters* (New York: Harper and Row, 1973), 8.

12. Selma Fraiberg, "Ghosts in the Nursery," in *Selected Writings of Selma Fraiberg*, ed. Louis Fraiberg (Columbus, Ohio: Ohio State University Press, 1987), 102.

Chapter 7: The Sister Knot

1. Toni A. H. McNaron, ed. *The Sister Bond: A Feminist View of a Timeless Connection* (New York: Pergamon Press, 1985), 7.

2. Ibid.

3. Ibid., 9-10.

4. Ibid., 10.

5. Ibid.

6. Diane D'Amico, "Maria: Christina Rosetti's Irreplaceable Sister and Friend," in *The Sister Bond: A Feminist View of a Timeless Connection*, ed. Toni A. H. McNaron (New York: Pergamon Press, 1985), 24.

7. O'Connor, *Friendships Between Women*, 158.

8. Eileen Simpson, *Orphans* (New York: Weidenfeld and Nicolson, 1987), 32-33.

9. O'Connor, *Friendships Between Women*, 159.

10. Ibid.

11. McNaron, *The Sister Bond*, 7.

12. Ibid., 8.

Chapter 8: Women and Friendship

1. Helen Gouldner and Mary Symons Strong, *Speaking of Friendship: Middle Class Women and Their Friends* (New York: Greenwood Press, 1987), 60 as quoted in O'Connor, *The Friendships of Women.*
2. Robert Bell, *Worlds of Friendship* (Beverly Hills, Calif.: Sage Publications, 1981), 65.
3. Ibid.
4. Joel Block, *Friendship: How to Give It, How to Get It* (New York: Collier, 1980), 53-55.
5. Ibid., 55.
6. Ibid., 56.
7. Ibid., 55.
8. Ibid., 56.
9. Rubenstein, "New Woman Survey," 78.
10. Bell, *Worlds of Friendship,* 58.
11. Block, *Friendship: How to Give It,* 29.
12. Ibid., 31.
13. Rubenstein, "New Woman Survey," 81.
14. O'Connor, *Friendships Between Women,* 17.
15. Ibid.
16. Ibid., 84.
17. Block, *Friendship: How to Give It,* 49.
18. Ibid., 50.
19. Ibid., 51.
20. Ibid., 52.
21. Shere Hite, *Women and Love* (New York: St. Martin's Press, 1989), 457.

Chapter 9: Key Players and Second Stringers

1. Judith Viorst, *Necessary Losses* (New York: Simon and Schuster, 1986), 180.
2. Ibid.
3. Ibid., 179-80.

4. C. S. Lewis, *The Four Loves* (New York: Harcourt, Brace, Jovanovich, 1960), 126.

Chapter 10: The Art of Friendship

1. Harville Hendrix, *Getting the Love You Want* (San Francisco: Harper Perennial, 1988), 93-94.
2. Jerry Authier, "Showing Warmth and Empathy," in *A Handbook of Communication Skills*, ed. Owen Hargie (Washington Square, N. Y.: New York University Press, 1986), 444-46.
3. Ibid., 449-50.
4. Viorst, *Necessary Losses*, 182.

Chapter 11: Surviving Conflict in Friendships

1. Sherryl Kleinman, *Social Forces* 67 (March 1989): 809-10.
2. Kim Bartholomew, "From Childhood to Adult Relationships: Attachment Theory and Research" in *Learning about Relationships*, vol. 2, ed. Steve Duck (Newbury Park, Calif.: Sage Publishers, 1992), 50.
3. Ibid.
4. Block, *Friendship: How to Give It*, 188-92.
5. Ibid.
6. Ibid., 191-92.

Chapter 12: Friendship's End

1. Dee Brestin, *The Joy of Women's Friendships* (Wheaton, Ill.: Victor Books, 1993), 21.
2. Michele Paludi, *The Psychology of Women* (Dubuque, Iowa: Brown and Benchmark, 1992), 180.
3. Susie Orbach and Luise Eichenbaum, *Bittersweet: Facing Up to Feelings of Love, Envy and Competition in Women's Friendships* (New York: Viking, 1987), 65.
4. Ibid., 81.

5. Steve Duck, *Repairing Personal Relationships*, vol. 5 of *Relationships* (New York: Academic Press, 1984), 167.
6. Viorst, *Necessary Losses, 182.*

Chapter 13: When Men Aren't Enough

1. Deborah Tannen, *You Just Don't Understand: Men and Women in Conversation* (New York: William Morrow, 1990), 23.
2. Josselson, *Finding Herself, 23.*
3. Ibid., 178.
4. Tannen, *You Just Don't Understand,* 76-77.
5. Ibid., 77.
6. Ibid., 81.

Chapter 14: Mentors: Passing the Torch

1. Belle Rose Ragins, "Barriers to Mentoring: The Female Manager's Dilemma," *Human Relations,* vol. 42, (January 1989): 2.
2. Ibid., 3.
3. Jan Johnson, "Mentor Me," *Virtue* (September/October 1993): 34.
4. Erik Erikson, *Childhood and Society* (New York: W. W. Norton and Company, 1964), 267.
5. Ibid., 268.
6. Virginia Duran, "Someday, You'll Do As Much," *Guideposts* (May 1994): 16.
7. Ruth 1:16.